# PEAK MODE

## 9 Tactical Concepts to Boost Productivity

BY

## Luis Amed Bustamante

# COPYRIGHTS

# Dedication

*To my daughter,*

*My love, my life, my light*

# Contents

Blank page

# **Preface**

Right off the bat, I must tell you that just choosing the name for this book was a challenge. I know you can imagine how the rest went. But I can also tell you that every challenge encountered while researching and writing was worth it. You know what they say, when you love what you do, you don't pay attention to the challenges, or something like that.

With all the doubts and ups and downs, I started creating what I call a productivity scheme to help you achieve your desired results using very simple concepts.

The simplest definition of **Productivity** is the relationship between the amount of effort and resources we employ in a specific process and the results obtained from it. So, now that we are aware of that relationship, we can agree that an increase in productivity occurs when we use less effort/resources and get equal results, or use the same effort/resources and obtain more results. With all that said, we can safely assume that most individuals and organizations are seeking to increase productivity in their daily activities. With this big desire, the next question is, *how can we achieve this increase in productivity?* Many books, training and articles have been developed to conquer this peak; many of those work well and others not so much.

But personally, I have always been a supporter of simplicity, and with that in mind, I present to you **PEAK MODE**. Allow me to introduce you to a set of 9 concepts that, once understood and put into action, will help you boost your productivity as an organization or individual as fast as 90 days. Here are 3 skills, 3 tools and 3 laws that will transform the way you acquire results.

At the time of writing this strategic book, I was about twelve months of switching my consulting field from Leadership to productivity. Before you ask, I would like to tell you why. See, number one, I support the concept that you should see what everybody is doing and then do something different; and at the time of my decision, there were too many consultants wrongly advising on leadership. Number two, according to Max DePree, "the first responsibility of a leader is to identify reality," and that is so true, and I also know that the main responsibility of a leader is to obtain results. With those two things in mind, I started developing more and more interest in how to multiply results. This took me to the path of *Business Productivity*.

I am sure that as you navigate these pages, you will find yourself with more knowledge to properly manage your resources and accommodate your efforts to obtain more

Results. Business productivity is rooted in how accurately you can create operational strategies and how soon you can set them into action. That is my true intention here, Ready Set Go.

# Introduction Entering Peak Mode

Every person, at some point in life, has asked themselves a simple yet powerful question: *How can I achieve more without burning out?* Some ask it after a long workday when nothing on the to-do list seems crossed off. Others ask it while running a business, juggling endless meetings, or chasing a dream that feels outs of reach. And some quietly ask it late at night, wondering why their efforts don't match the results they see others achieving.

The pursuit of productivity is universal. From the dawn of civilization, humans have been striving to do more with less, less time, fewer resources, less energy. Farmers once invented irrigation systems to increase their yield. Explorers created maps to save time and prevent wasted journeys. Modern technology, from the printing press to artificial intelligence, was born out of the need to multiply output while minimizing input.

And yet, despite centuries of progress, we still find ourselves struggling. We live in an age of unprecedented opportunity and endless resources, but we are also drowning in distractions, overstimulation, and overwhelm. In the past, people competed against scarcity; today, we compete against abundance. We have more tools, more choices, and more information than ever before, but sometimes, that abundance paralyzes us instead of empowering us.

**Peak Mode** was created to cut through the noise. It is a framework, a strategy, and a philosophy all in one. It is not about working longer hours, chasing every opportunity, or subscribing to another "hack" that only lasts a week. It is about entering a state of clarity and execution where every decision, every effort, and every action serves your highest priorities.

## Why Productivity Matters More Than Ever

Think about your average day. How many times do you check your phone? How many emails pull you in different directions? How often do you start one task only to abandon it halfway through because another one demanded your attention? If this sounds familiar, you're not alone. Research shows the average person spends nearly half their workday on unplanned tasks and distractions. That means half of our potential is wasted before we even realize it.

The cost of low productivity is not just professional, it is personal. Unfinished projects lead to frustration. Poor time usage creates stress that bleeds into our families and relationships. A lack of structure and systems erodes confidence, leaving us wondering if we are capable of more. But the opposite is also true. When you unlock productivity, life begins to expand. Suddenly, you are not simply reacting, you are directing. You're not just busy, you're effective. You're not living on autopilot, you're designing your days with intention. Productivity is not just about getting more done; it's about creating space for what matters most. It gives you the power to balance ambition with peace of mind, achievement with fulfillment, and success with significance.

**The Peak Mode Philosophy**

At its core, **Peak Mode** is about one guiding principle: *simplicity with impact.* Complexity kills execution. If a strategy requires dozens of moving pieces, you won't stick with it. But if it's simple enough to understand and apply, it becomes part of your daily rhythm.

That's why this book is built around nine tactical concepts divided into three essential groups:

1. **The Skills** – Personal competencies every individual must master:

   o **Goal Setting** – clarifying your "why" and building the roadmap.

   o **Time Usage** – mastering your most valuable resource.

- **Project Management** – structuring efforts for maximum results.

2. **The Tools** – External systems that bring structure and accountability:

   - **Checklists** – eliminating forgetfulness and chaos.

   - **SOPs (Standard Operating Procedures)** – creating consistency.

   - **KPIs (Key Performance Indicators)** – measuring what matters.

3. **The Laws** – Timeless principles that govern outcomes:

   - **Law of Averages** – results are built by repetition.

   - **Law of Diminishing Intent** – act before enthusiasm fades.

   - **Law of Cause and Effect** – everything produces a consequence.

   - These nine concepts are not random; they are deliberate building blocks. Together, they form a system that can be applied by individuals, teams, and organizations alike. They don't just improve productivity in theory, they transform results in practice.

## What Makes Peak Mode Different

There's no shortage of books on productivity. Some will fire you up with motivational stories, others bury you under complex frameworks. **Peak Mode** stands apart because it bridges both worlds. It recognizes that productivity is both **internal** and **external**:

- The *internal game*, your mindset, discipline, focus, and resilience.

- The *external game*, the tools, structures, and measurements that keep you accountable.

Most people fail because they master one side but neglect the other. They're motivated but disorganized. Or they have great systems but no drive. Peak Mode aligns both.

Another unique quality is its **scalability**. Whether you are a student, a solo entrepreneur, a manager leading a team, or an executive steering an entire organization, the same nine concepts apply. You'll find yourself able to adapt the principles to your specific context, whether that means finishing a personal project, launching a new business, or scaling operations.

And perhaps most importantly, **Peak Mode is built for action.** You will not simply read and nod, you will do. Each concept invites you to put pen to paper, to test ideas, to create systems, and to measure results. Productivity is not a spectator sport. It is a practice, and this book will keep you moving.

## The Cost of Staying the Same

Before diving into the system, let's pause for an uncomfortable truth: if you keep doing what you've been doing, you'll keep getting what you've been getting.

Every day you delay creating structure, you lose precious time. Every time you procrastinate, you pay in stress later. Every time you avoid clarity, you pay in confusion and wasted energy. Productivity is not just about earning more money or completing more tasks, it's about reclaiming your life from chaos.

Think of it this way: five years from now, you will arrive somewhere. The question is, *where*? Will you drift into the future with regrets, or will you arrive at a destination you intentionally designed? That choice begins today.

## How to Use This Book

This is not a book to be skimmed once and shelved. It is a manual, a reference, and a guide. Here's how to get the most from it:

1. **Read with intention.** Don't rush. Let each concept sink in and imagine how it applies to your life.

2. **Apply immediately.** After finishing a chapter, take one small action. Productivity compounds when practiced.

3. **Adapt to your context.** Whether you're an individual or part of a large organization, mold the concepts to your needs.

4. **Review and repeat.** This book is designed to be revisited. When you feel stuck, return to the fundamentals.

## The Results You Can Expect

If you commit to this journey, here's what will begin to shift in your life:

- You will no longer confuse being busy with being productive.

- Your goals will transform from vague dreams into clear, measurable plans.

- You'll stop reacting to your schedule and start designing it.

- Projects that once felt overwhelming will be broken into achievable steps.

- You'll measure your growth with clarity instead of guessing.

- Most importantly, you'll experience the freedom that comes from being in control of your time, energy, and results.

This is what it means to live in **Peak Mode**, to operate at your highest level with consistency, clarity, and confidence.

**A Final Word Before We Begin**

This book is not about perfection, it is about progress. You will not become flawlessly productive overnight. You will slip, get distracted, or fall into old habits at times. That's not failure, that's reality. What matters is that you recommit, reset, and move forward.

Remember this: productivity is not a skill for the few. It is not reserved for CEOs, athletes, or high performers. It is a choice, a decision to live with intention rather than drift. If you can commit to practicing these concepts, you will not only achieve more, but you will also transform the way you live.

So, take a deep breath, clear your mind, and prepare yourself. The climb toward peak performance begins here. And the view from the top will be worth every step.

Welcome to **Peak Mode.**

# Section I. The Skills

These are a combination of hard and soft skills that will elevate your performance in no time. I will tell you that, as with everything else in life, the more you practice them, the better you get at them. With that said, there are three **skills** that every person must learn to be able to increase productivity and obtain their desired results faster. These skills are Goal Setting, Time Usage and Project Management. Let's get to know them better.

# Chapter One: Goal Setting

If you do not have a goal, you do not have a **WHY** and of course, you will not even know how. Mr. Jim Rohn said that "you can either make a living or design a life." To design that life, you will have to intentionally and periodically set goals. You will need to clearly understand that to get more results, you must first set goals directed towards those results. Every successful person will tell you that the goal- setting part of their life was very exhausting but very remunerative at the same time. An organization or person with clear goals will eventually see that reflected in their personal finance or company cash flow.

Setting goals keeps you motivated; they bring uncertainty and excitement to your life. Goal setting sits among the most important skills to have when looking into increasing production. And here is how you properly do it:

**<u>Renew your Mindset!</u>**

You are now on a path of growth and fully committed to obtaining the results you desired for a long time. Be aware that to achieve these results, you must alter your activities; to alter those activities, you must adjust the plan; but before you can change the plan, you must change your mind. The way you see life is the biggest influencer on your behavior.

Everything starts in the brain; there is no difference when it comes to productivity. This commitment to do things differently and grow intentionally must start in the brain. Here, I share some strategies I often teach to positively alter your mindset.

***Believe:***

Believing that you can increase your productivity is very motivating, but to finally do it might be a very frustrating task, because this is one of those things that is easier said than done. As I mentioned, results won't change overnight, but there is a way to conquer these beliefs, and that is **awareness.** I call it "The retroactive awareness" to increase your results:

*Your results are altered by your actions, but your actions are altered by your decisions - your decisions are altered by your thoughts - your thoughts are altered by your beliefs, and beliefs are directly influenced by:*

***Background:*** *The events you had experienced, where you were raised, and the schools you went to.*

***Environment:*** *Your workplace, where you often hang out, and your neighborhood.*

***Repetition of information:*** *What you often listen to and watch, social media search history.*

**_Reliable sources:_** *it is often teachers, professors, friends and these days, social media.*

*Attitude:*

How do you perceive life? From what energy pole do you approach daily events? A positive attitude is vital to produce incredible results. There is no talent that can win over the right attitude. I would like to refer to this concept early in the scheme because you will need it all along the way. I know you heard before that the right attitude defines your altitude, then you must ensure that you, or if applicable, your TEAM, have the right attitude most of the time. You might not have 100 percent days every day, but you should have a 100 percent attitude all the time.

I know you heard the story of The Donkey in the hole before; this story is a perfect example of the importance of a positive attitude:

A man's donkey fell into a deep pit and, thinking that it would be impossible to retrieve his donkey from the bottom of the pit, he decided to bury it alive. As the soil was poured in, the donkey shook it off its back and stepped on it, repeating this process as more soil was added.

Eventually, the donkey rose above the pit and was grazing in green pastures.

This illustrates how one can overcome challenges by shaking off the negativity and using problems as stepping stones. The right attitude often will help you approach challenges and setbacks with a focus on possibilities and solutions rather than dwelling on negativity. This soft skill is part of a resilient mind, and you and I can agree on how important resiliency is when trying to achieve our goals.

### *Abundance:*

Increase productivity and big results, is that what you are aiming at, right? And we are here together to achieve that, right? If I ask if you believe in the law of attraction, what would be your response? No worries, I will share my response with you. I do believe that a big mindset attracts big results and big things into our lives. It is something like if you aim at the moon and miss, you at least be in the sky.

President Donald J. Trump was right when he said, "You have to think anyway, so why not think big?" You must believe deep in your heart that out there are unlimited resources and opportunities to accomplish your goals. And unlike a scarcity mindset, know that these resources and opportunities are yours to use without anyone's permission. It is understandable that doubts will appear at times and situations, and yes, this is normal for every go-getter and dreamer, but you must dream big and send the bill to GOD.

I know for a fact he can pay for it. You promptly realize that your faith plays a crucial role in your path to goal accomplishment.

Like I often mention, there is absolutely nothing wrong with big goals; don't let anyone make you feel bad for wanting to become a millionaire, an astronaut, a neurosurgeon, a professional athlete, or else. Big goals make you dream big and elevate your mindset where small minds can't reach. So yes, be careful with whom you share these goals; small minds will never understand them and will call them impossible, and even more dangerously, they will try to convince you that you can't do it. So, when it comes to an abundance of mind, my best advice is to protect your bubble and keep growing. And if you ask me how to create and keep that mentality? I will say that the easiest way to create a mentality of abundance is to practice consistent gratitude and vast service to others. In addition to belief, attitude, and abundance, there are two more powerful mindset tools that will push your goals forward: discipline and visualization.

## Discipline: The clandestine VIP of Your Objectives

Most individuals make resolutions and almost none can accomplish them. Why? Do you know why? They overlook the discipline, which is a secret ingredient. Discipline is whatever you have to do when you do not want to do it. Any and all of the best athletes, best scientists, and best entrepreneurs will tell you that talent or intelligence might show you a head start, but it is only discipline that will bring you to the finish line. Consider a bodybuilder: it is not difficult to lay out the desired result (lifting 100kg), but it is hard to walk down there, work hard every time, eat properly, and sleep well; that is discipline. Without discipline, a dream is just a dream.

## Visualization: See It Before You Live It

The visualization is one of the potent gadgets in goal setting your brain could not tell a vividly imagined thing apart from a real one. Visualization is why professional athletes tend to use it to practice notable events. Olympic swimmer Michael Phelps also admitted to visualizing his races in every aspect in his mind more than 20,000 times before the competitions. When real race came, his body was only implementing what his mind had already practiced. Imagine yourself reaching your goal every morning-spend five minutes and make it clear in your mind-think about it five minutes every morning-feel it, see it and hear it. This becomes a confidence-building, strengthening belief system practice.

## <u>Sharpens your Focus!</u>

You probably have a good number of goals and along those goals, you might have multiple resources to manage; also, ideas may be flowing through your mind like a river. I know because I have been in your position, and to be honest, it still happens to me. To manage these things going on at the same time, it requires you need to maintain a high level of focus. Productivity consultant David Allen accurately affirms that we do not need more time; we need more focus and control over the key activities.

Every time I must elevate my level of focus, I pay more attention to these three areas:

***Concentration***: The ability to concentrate on one task at a time is important to increase productivity. A mind that fails to concentrate is an undisciplined mind. With that said, we can agree that this modern world is full of distractions. We can blame many sources for this issue, but at the end of the day, it is our responsibility to maintain our focus on the end goal.

In an article called "Can People Really Multitask?" Adam Chris wrote, "When you think you are multitasking, you are switching your goals and turning the respective brain rules from task to task on and off in rapid succession". That means you aren't ALL IN; you were never actually committed. Do not get me wrong, you might be able to get stuff done, but not to increase your productivity. Multitasking at work is like texting and driving; you might get to the destination, but at what cost? And can you keep doing it over and over for a long period of time? There are multiple functional exercises to practice and increase your concentration. I highly encourage you to jump into some of those if the shoe fits and it probably does.

***Clearness*:** Clarity is a requisite for focus, as clearness is related to understanding. The clearer the vision, the better it is to see the finish line; the clearer the vision, the easier it is to share it with others. It is a fact that to increase results, you will need others to buy into your vision. You will need human resources to achieve your goals and to obtain the best performance from the team of people helping you. You will need to share the vision with them.

"Write the vision and make it plain, so he who reads it runs towards it" Habakkuk 2:2

A clear vision is easier to understand and so it helps create a clear message to share. Achievers are leaders and leaders are communicators. As a good leader, you should know that the elements of good communication are conciseness, consistency, and **clarity**. Imagine you and/or your team having a clear understanding of the organizational vision, the mission and the values? Sounds great, right? Just remember that the clearer the path, the higher the energy concentration towards the goals.

***Competence***: We are all expecting you to be the Subject matter expert, and you could stay as the expert by keeping the relevance in your field. I am a full supporter of lifelong learning, either with new subjects or updating existing knowledge. No matter which one it is, perpetual learning helps you to stay relevant in your industry, in shape with your field of expertise.

There is no better way for a person or organization to decrease productivity than not to stay in constant development with their industry environment. I am sure you are familiar with stories like Kodak or Blockbuster. The disappearance of these big organizations was only because their leadership refused to stay relevant and competent with their operation in relation to the direction in which the future was going.

Paying attention and awareness are very important for success. With the number of distractors in our environment, it becomes almost impossible to stay focused. Studies show that the attention span of the average person declined from 12 seconds in 2000 to 8.25 seconds in 2025. These types of facts are your signs to increase and sharpen your focus. Many can still not manage to be consistent or feel overwhelmed, even with great concentration. Here is where micro-goals and accountability are life-transforming.

## Accountability: Never Walk alone

Accountability is also a very effective strategy. When you make a promise to yourself, you can easily break it; however, when it comes to a promise to another person, it is difficult. That is why an accountability partner, coach, or mentor can get you well ahead of schedule. In cases where there is someone who takes note of your improvement, you tend to work harder. Suppose you have made a commitment to wake up at 5 to make it into the gym, and you suspect your friend will be waiting in the park- chances are, you will rise up.

Responsibility transforms objectives into promises.

## Micro-Goals: tiny victories, enormous triumphs

There are times when ambitious goals may be too great to handle and one may as well end up procrastinating. To counter this, they have to be split up into micro-goals. In other words, instead of saying, I will write a book this year, say, I will write 500 words a day. All these presumed small wins compound, compound and eventually deliver huge outputs. Consider anyone who climbs up a mountain--they do not take giant leaps and bound all the way up to the very top. They make small steps, but each small step takes them one step nearer the peak. Micro-goals avoid burnout, and they keep you on track.

## **Be S.M.A.R.T**

In 1981, Jim Doran introduced the world to an incredible concept during a management meeting, a concept that is now responsible for multiple organizational achievements. This concept is so simple and accurate that a middle school kid can apply it and triumph. These days, the SMART analogy for goals has been responsible for vision/mission achievement all over the world and in all areas of life, from fitness to financial to spiritual. Here is how to be **productive SMART.**

*Specific:* It is perfectly ok to have big goals, but they must be very specific. Specific set goals give you a better view of the resources needed to achieve them. If the content of your goal is too wide, it may cause confusion to a team or complicate the planning process. Therefore, specifications and clarity of vision are a vital part of your goal-setting process. A prime example is if you ask a high schooler what is your goal? He or she might answer as "Go to college". But which college? What field of study? Where? Etc. Specificity is equal to clearness.

*Measurable*: Your success will always be judged based on your results. I always heard people say that "success is a numbers game". This is why you must be able to measure everything you do within your operations. What gets measured gets accomplished. Every time you use a resource from your resource tool bag (time, money, skill), you should measure it against the result before using it. One of the best allies of the measurement department is timelines (start dates, follow-ups, end dates, etc.)

*Attainable*: Again, there is nothing wrong with big goals, but it is important to stay within realistic borders when setting your goals. You should ask yourself, are your resources capable of fulfilling the tasks to gain the results you expect?

During this attainable part of the goal-setting process, you must be extremely honest with yourself, because one overrated resource can delay and even stop the operation of a project.

**Relevant:** A direct and clear relationship between the vision, the process, and the resources available is vital to accomplish your goals. This is the best way to maintain relevancy with your goals. When your goals are relevant to your daily activities, it increases the odds of accomplishing them because of the law of association.

**Time bound**: There is something special about dates; they can transform a regular moment into and memorable event; think about birth dates, for example. When you set a start date for your project, it creates motivation. And when you put an end date on your goal, you create a sense of urgency and excitement to achieve it. The gap between those dates is the most important time-bound period during that moment. Although SMART goals provide you with the structure, make it a habit: always know that there is flexibility and celebration, which can ensure long-term success.

## Flexibility: Not the goal, but the Sail should be altered

Life is not that predictable and plans do not always work. That does not imply that the objective was not proper; it just implies that you need to modify the approach. A sailor does not have the power to determine the direction that the wind blows, but he always has the ability to maneuver his sails to achieve the destination. Flexibility enables you to go with the wind without quitting. Keep in mind that failure is not the antidote to success; failure is a component of success. All failure is mere feedback advising you on how to change strategies.

## Celebration: Rewards the Journey

Many people celebrate when they finally achieve the main objective, but this attitude destroys motivation. You will have to know how to celebrate minor victories on the way. Treat rewards when you complete major milestones- this feels motivating to the brain. The feel-good hormone (dopamine) also boosts our desire to persist when we realize we have made some progress. An example follows; in case you want to participate in a marathon, then you should celebrate the accomplishments that you have run your first 5 km, 10 km, and so on. It is not a one-time experience that involves progress.

# Chapter Two: Time Usage

So far, there is no doubt that you have numerous resources that can help support your goals. I would like to briefly tell my observation on how I have been dealing with our greatest resource in delivering the results and that is time.

Have you ever experienced a moment when you were savoring the moment when you feel time is passing more slowly, as compared to when you are bored? Have you ever experienced a time seems to pass quickly, when you sense that you are losing it? Those are not tricky questions at all, but the phenomenon occurs more frequently in individuals who do not pay respect to the authority of time. So the first thing is you need to know that you cannot manage time; all you can do is manage how you utilize your own time. In that light, we can now agree that as human beings we do things as we feel and that we give our best in things that we feel the most; it is then categorically clear that we put our values priority on what we focus on hence making whatever we prioritize consumes our most valuable asset which in this case is time.

Regarding prioritizing, we need to revert to the applicable part of SMART goals. All the activities that you engage in should be relevant to your intentions. The most helpful piece of advice I can give you in order to better use your time is to avoid involvement in anything that does not correlate with your final aims. So you need to do your duty and do it when duty must be done.

Rory Vaden introduced us to the idea of 3D thinking, and the idea, inside, helps us to define the prioritization of things and the idea also moves us to act and make things work better.

- **Urgency:** The soon-to-be-important time.
- **Importance:** What is the degree of importance?
- **Significance:** The duration will be of importance.

We should tackle this a bit further, since this straightforward idea is a revelation. A high-priority task may be an emergency because it screams in your ear like a phone, but its significance may be quite low. An activity of great significance, such as getting ready to offer a major presentation, may not be pressing this morning, but the effect it has on your career is enormous. And this dimension of Significance is the worst attended as well. An example of a significant action such as a task is a task such as a delegation of a repetitive project. It may require time and energy at the outset (because it does not seem to be as urgent and important as your deadline), but once it happens, you will save your time and energy in the following weeks, months, or even years. It is not just on what is urgent or important that you should be spending most of your time, but on what has the greatest Significance. It is about making investments of time, not spending.

One cannot save or create more time; we all have the same amount of it, so you can only do what you can with it by utilizing it properly. Three things that you should do to use your time accurately are described below:

## Planning

Upon straightening up your priorities, this step will assist you in using your time accurately. One must be careful when planning, one must work when planning and planning takes time, but the value of planning is to be taken with a lot of seriousness and way overemphasized.

This is most likely not a new idea to you: Proper Planning Prevents Poor Performance; now you know all about planning, the famous 5 Ps. Most of the time and mental energy is consumed during the planning of any project because it is sensitive and critical. This is precisely the reason why many are unwilling to do it and this is the same carelessness that results in failure.

Benjamin Franklin said, *if you do not plan, you are planning to fail.*

So, you make planning easy:

The initial point is that one must think on paper; one must be aware that when it is not on paper, there is no plan. Although powerful as he is, no brain is supposed to carry the burden of a plan and how to work on it alone. It should be the work of the brain to execute the idea, the plan of the paper. It has been proven that those who set their goals in paper have 42 percent higher chances of accomplishing their goals. When you write a plan, it adds more clarity to the planning process and illuminates the pathway to success.

Secondly, task/ sub-task each segment of your big project. In this way, you will be able to look at it more clearly and feel the joy of little improvements. The length of tasks that are required to get the mission done is dependent on the size of the project. Other times, the breakdown into subtasks may be enormous and you cannot afford NOT to break it down. You have heard the saying, how do you eat an elephant, one bite at a time.

Let us consider a large goal such as "Start a successful online business." This is one monster objective. Once it is on paper, it becomes smaller and doable. These elements are: You must create a business plan, develop a product, build a site and launch a marketing campaign. Any of these is still a huge task now. And you collapse them in your turn. The phrase "Build a website" changes to the form's line, "Choose a platform," "Write the content of 5 pages," Write the logo, the mechanism of payment. That is the way it is. Breaking it down, you generate a step-by-step blueprint, and you eliminate the feeling of being overwhelmed before a person even starts.

The third one is alright to plan on the GO. But at times we do want to inject immediate actions in our mind and trust me, at times we should. General planning, rapid, and then prolonging the phase of the plan in the movement, it is necessary to exploit time and movement. And naturally, so much of the planning is the follow-up. Such follow-ups are essential not only because you have to be in a position to follow the progress, but more importantly, to know whether there is no progress. Such follow-ups will enable you to look at the plan and the objectives. Figuratively, are you getting the bullseye with your bullets? You want and need to know the answer to this question.

## The Problem of Procrastination

One hopes to have the best plan ever, but the worst killer of productivity is procrastination. It is a sense of delaying the time to act, because of the perfect moment or not having yet a correct motivation (which does not come along). But have a secret to tell you: You do not approach motivation to work; you work to achieve motivation. An object that is moving will continue to move. When something is bigger than you can handle, do not think of the entire situation. All you have to do is just take the very first, the smallest step. The inertia of that step, so slight, has in many cases been sufficient to bring you the rest of the way. As you know, the road to a thousand miles starts with one step.

Time blocking is one of the strongest methods to fight procrastination. Rather than a long checklist, you physically declared certain periods in your calendar reserved for certain activities. As an example, between 9:00 AM and 10:00 AM, there is the activity Writing Chapter Two. Between 10.00 AM and 10.30 AM, there is the Responding to Emails. This way, you have to engage in a certain task over a certain time and this narrows down the cognitive tension of what to do next. It turns your to-do list into a goal-oriented, implementable plan.

## Battle Rhythm – Standards – Hierarchy

About 40 of the 500 Fortune 500 Company CEOs are of military background. You will be thinking of leadership and discipline, but I will extend the thought to include Battle Rhythm, Standards and Hierarchy. So, let us say something about these 3 components.

## Battle Rhythm: The Power of Consistency

We can all agree that we are creatures of habit and when it comes to the most important aspects of our lives, we like to have consistency. What I like about military activities, assuming that there is something in the military worth liking, is the sequence of activities taking place periodically by date and time, what we call in the Army Battle Rhythm. This established list of tasking creates the consistency that is necessary to drive productivity out of the same resources.

As an instance, your weekly meeting with your team occurs at 8.00 am every Monday, your budget review is scheduled every 3rd of each month, the marketing strategies are observed every three months (90 days), etc. Breakdown of quarterly, monthly, and weekly tasking is possible with this system. This gives you and the team member's greater control over individual/ organization events and the schedule. This regulation can be directly converted to a more comfortable place of work and we all know that a comfortable worker is a productive worker.

The rhythms of battles and other similar equipment have been tried as a source of stress reduction since the uncertainty is also less. When supervisors use this tool, they will be less prone to micromanagement. Nobody enjoys the feel of constant supervisory stress, which is not good for anyone in the team. Everyone is living in a battle rhythm they are all familiar with and is managing deadlines, meetings and expectations. In combination with other tools you would acquire during this reading journey, the battle rhythm and schedule will assist you in predicting the outcomes and identifying the progress more easily.

One of the most powerful things you can do when doing this is creating a personal or a team battle rhythm. It is the removal of guessing in your day-to-day tasks. Consider your morning routine: you wake up every morning at 6.00 am, review the three most important things you need to accomplish each day at 6.15 and then you will do the hardest thing at 6.30. This daily cadence will make sure you are working on the most important, rather than what is urgent.

The delegation process is also trickier in this system, as a repetitive task can be delegated with confidence that the other person is aware of the timing the task should be accomplished.

**Standards: The DNA of Quality**

Well-laid standards are the most significant in the procedural development of an organization. Automated systems have their origin in standards, and all parts of the systems stand on standards. operation. This is why the kind of outcomes that you are obtaining is either what you hoped to get or it is dependent on what is expected of you.

Standards are habits that contribute to the formation of organizational culture. Such a culture enables the organization to operate in a stable environment.

I can promise that properly established standards will improve your time utilization and enhance your skill in goal setting. The efficiency will vanish in case you do not standardize one of your operations. Consistency and commitment are required to standardize something.

Consider a rather easy combination. Otherwise (not adhering to the recipe, the standard), your food will never taste the same way. However, with accurate measurements and adherence to products and directions, uniformity is achieved.

Such is the strength of standards. They do away with variables and the result is predictable of high prediction.

Stabilization advantages are, among others:

- **Create Certainty:** No one is left in doubt of what is required.
- **Consistency:** The end result or product is never varied.
- **Predict Results:** You are able to predict with a greater level of accuracy.
- **Safety:** It assures you and your team of safety against mistakes.

This is why I so much respect Standards Operating Procedures (SOP). They comprise the fruits and vegetables of any operation. A greater degree of SOPs will be covered in the upcoming section of the book.

**Hierarchy: The Power of Priorities**

The most prolific work groups establish a pyramid-style organization of everyone's position in the latter. Standards and battle rhythms, among others, are very important factors in the functioning of any given organization, together with a well-established hierarchy. When we speak about productivity, the hierarchical order of the three following elements is also crucial.

- **Achievements:** What are the first things you will have to record?
- **Resources:** What will you require and in what sequence?
- **Actions:** What should be your first steps?

When one says: Do not do that which is easiest or most difficult: do first that which ought to be done: but what he really means is, when he says so: Do not do what is easiest first or what is hardest first, but what ought to be first.

Hierarchical structure is more efficient, the decision-making process as well as the accountability is leaner to manage, and the flow of communication is more focused.

A good example of a hierarchy of productivity is the Pareto Principle or the 80/20 Rule. It puts it in simple terms that 80 per cent of your outcome is with 20 per cent of your inputs. It is your task to find that 20 percent and address it with everyday priority. This implies telling no to 80 percent of the activities that have trivial output. It is quite an easy rule, but it is one of the hardest ones to follow, as it makes you stare at the fact that not every fix or every job is equal. The most efficient individuals and corporations do what is most needed first, end of story. They realize that a few activities in particular will yield a high percentage of what they want.

Your day, the week and your projects are hierarchically organized, and this is the very structure of your productivity. The roadmap helps you not waste your time and efforts on worthless activities. Your prioritization needs to be brutal and your ability to stop and ask yourself the question: Is this the most impactful thing I can be doing at the moment?

Using these three elements, Battle Rhythm, Standards and Hierarchy, you can change the concept of relationship with time and you move it to the concept of intention rather than reaction. You are no longer a servant to the clock because you are the master. Your goals, not the clock, determine your life.

**The Art of Saying NO**

Since we have already discussed the importance of prioritizing what you get to do, it would only be fair to ensure we touch lightly on the other side of the coin, saying NO to things you do not need to do. When I say no, it is not about being hard, but rather it is a way of preserving the most important thing that you have, which is time. You are saying no to goals each time you say yes to something not in line with your goals. Examples of mastery of saying no include being the most productive people in the world. They are focused on the future, as well as having a specific list of priorities; anything beyond these priorities is diplomatically but nevertheless strenuously refused. It is self-discipline and self-respect.

Reasons people would not say no most often include having a fear of conflict, being a people-pleaser, and not being clear about what the person wants. By getting control of your goals (Chapter One) and your time (Chapter Two), you provide yourself with a solid basis out of which to make these tough choices. No longer are you responding to the world; now you are operating out of your vision.

**Embracing the Follow-Up Culture**

We said something about follow-ups above, but I would like to go into more detail about why this is so important. A follow-up is not only a reminder; it is also solidifying your goals. It is an hour of responsibility. It is the process of asking yourself to be truthful in the question of whether something is working. That is where the value of a regular follow-up calendar comes in; it balances the see-saw. A moving vessel acts in a manner that continuously corrects the course of direction on a voyage toward its destination, given the wind and the currents, as well as the vessel's location. A follow-through will make the difference between a rudderless ship and a fruitful voyage.

The system I would recommend to you is the regular follow- up system. In the case of a large project, this will be a weekly check-in. In the case of a personal goal, it could be the weekly review of your progress. Do not waste such time wallowing in self-recrimination, but use it to educate yourself. When you are not happy, what is it that is not functioning, then you have the chance to alter it? A feedback loop is an essential component of your success, which is your follow-up system. This process of inspection and correction is what separates the folks who improve and those who stagnate.

## The Myth of Perfectionism

And finally, we should discuss the productivity assassin, perfectionism. Seeking perfection can be a sort of highfalutin procrastination. We have given ourselves time to wait, time to plan, time to wait again and thereby we will never act. A terrific strategy implemented now is superior to an excellent strategy in one week's time. You have to realize that the aim is to move forward and not to perfection. The most major achievers of the world have understood how to unleash less than perfect action. They also understand that they will be able to modify and better during the process. It is like the contrast between attempting to make a perfect car out of an initial bolt and merely getting a car that works on the road and then steadily modifying it.

I cannot afford the time to be spent in the paralysis of perfectionism. Acquire the ability to accept the good enough for now attitude. This does not imply that you are supposed to go low. It becomes known that you must be ready to take action and do better along the way.

Using the principles of the entire 3D thinking model that involves applying these insights into the power of follow-ups and the benefits of rejecting perfectionism will ensure that your time will no longer become a stress, but an asset that can bring you the desired results. The thing is that everybody has 24 hours a day. The only divide between the users and the non-users is how they utilize them. Choose productively.

# Chapter Three: Project management

Do you feel that it is a big deal (be the one responsible) in terms of the whole project? Do you feel you would be capable of that responsibility? I asked such questions because whatever your objective may be, it is your project, and you are the manager. It does not matter how big it is, small, medium, or large, a project and whether the goal is to launch a new strategy of business strategy, develop new technologies, build a house, or simply lose weight. Whatever the project, it is yours; you are the one who must make it happen, and don't get all tensed up. Here is how you do it.

Project management involves nothing more than leadership abilities. It does not really matter which region in the world you live in; it does not matter whether a leader is good or bad, as long as they can bring results that is the primary responsibility of a leader. In order to achieve such outcomes, the individual who has responsibility should be effective in utilizing all the resources that are at his/her disposal. And the lack of project management skills contributes to an astonishingly high 70 percent of all projects failing to achieve their objective. Project management is all about knowing where your resources are and, in what particular case, they should be apportioned in order to achieve those results.

I still confess that the most enjoyable stage of any project is to have … done and that is what project managers do every day. You should understand that in order to manage any project effectively, you will concentrate on three issues:

**Budget:** What amount of money will you have available to undertake the project and to which you will allocate that money to obtain other resources (Technology, people, etc.) and the frequency and the quantity with which you will use the resource. Any amount that is over can ruin the entire project.

**Schedule:** What is the number of working days/days left or the amount of time to ensure that the entire project is done? Make a **breakdown of times by tasks.**

**Scope:** What are all the tasks required and specific requirements to undertake in order to get this project finished?

When we are able to have a close tie between these three dimensions, we have ensured excellent results throughout. In the project management world, these three are referred to as the Triple Constraint. They form a triangle because there is a reason why you cannot alter one without influencing the other. You can do that to expand the range of your project, but it will require more time or more money, or both. Since you would be forced to make budgetary reductions, you either have to cut the scope or the schedule. This is one of the basic, but effective ideas of any successful project.

In order to bring out your project management capabilities then you need another ideology that you need to put in your head. It is Movement and Maneuver; I took this idea when I was serving in the US Army, since it demonstrates to service members how to traverse the battlefield. The growth of this ideology will take a different shape in this book, yet it will educate you on how to maneuver in order to enhance your project management ability and ensure your deliverables. He does it this way:

**Bold Decisions**

What does it require to be confident enough and go outside our comfort zone? Between fight or flight, how is the difference in a split second? Say what it is, say it is a decision. The point of making or breaking to make your results multiply needs to be literally the decision, as an example, you decided to read this book to improve your productivity. I am aware that one cannot make all decisions, but I am certain that even then, the worst decision is the one that you do not take. I would like to capture, just like in your own mind, a visual picture of just why decisions are so very important. Consider a situation when you manage to get into an elevator, but you do not push any buttons. What will most likely be the result? Yes, and the elevator will either remain on the same floor or go somewhere somebody else asked it to. That is the large issue of dragging on too long, or not deciding at all.

The principal obstacle to making decisions is uncertainty; people are not comfortable making a decision when they cannot predict the consequences of the event. Consider the choice when deciding to clean your teeth in the morning, you certainly are aware that the result when you fail to clean them will be bad breath, and this will be noticed by others, a bad profile of yours. In the instance of such an example, you know instinctively, designation so that you respond and brush your teeth.

The logical question is now, how do you make sure you make better decisions? I got acquainted with several strategies that can help to maximize the probability of making a correct decision.

First, I will make the assumption that you realize that to lose the fear of deciding, you must be more certain than ever about the consequences of your decision, or must be able to foresee them. There is no better way of doing that than being and remaining the subject matter expert. The trick to getting as close to the optimal decision as possible is perpetual learning to make you the most exposed to the future results.

The second approach is to ensure that we make the right decision. I read somewhere that one wise man once said, You are going to succeed, because you make good decisions, and one way to know how to make good decisions is to make bad decisions. No, there is a more sensible way. I simply took the steps from the Military Decision-Making Process and slightly modified it to work with project management.

**Accept Challenge:** This is to make a goal/ relate to the project and stick to it.

**Tasks and Resources Analysis:** Examine all the scopes required and know all the tools that are available to use.

**Make plans of action:** Develop some alternative schemes for attaining your goal.

**Compare & Choose a Plan of Action:** Read the possible scenarios of each plan of action, compare the strengths and weaknesses and adhere to the most realistic and applicable.

**Implement Decision:** Take all actions to the final decision. Let us see how this is applicable in a real-life situation. Your imagination has to be that you have a project to launch a new fitness app.

**Take on The Challenge:** You choose that this is your project; this is your call. You take a risk competing in a hard market.

**Analyze Tasks and Resources:** You list all the tasks: market research, find a developer, design the user interface, create content, and marketing. You are aware of what resources you have: 50 thousand dollars of budget and three people in a group.

**Develop Plans of Action:** You think of some plans of action.

> Plan A: Get a full-stack developer and create the app from scratch.

> Plan B: Apply a no-code platform and an outsourced team.

> Plan C: Make a simpler version (called a Minimum Viable Product) and add the features in between.

**Compare & Choose a Plan:** You consider the advantages and disadvantages. Plan A is costly and takes time, but it is fully controlled. Plan B is also quicker and less customizable. The most realistic plan would be Plan C, as it is the quickest and would fit into your budget. You select Plan C.

**Decision Take Action:** You begin at once to produce the minimum viable product. You don't fall into analysis paralysis, you do.

I know you will not necessarily have the time to go through this process in every circumstance, but at least the most crucial ones will. In instances where quick decisions need to be made, you will need to operate on the basis of common sense, previous experiences and knowledge gained. Other recommendations to make decisions within a reasonable time are: Minimize the level of uncertainty, limit the number of choices that may be offered and never forget that the worst action is the step you never made.

**Consistent Actions**

You have just figured out that it is not as simple as snapping your fingers in order to decide. However, when you believe that was difficult, you have to know the tech, this aspect of movement and maneuver, step five in the decision-making process. When this is done, you enter the most difficult part. There are a few things not strictly essential where productivity is concerned; one of the most pertinent is regular, big action. Sustained consistency leads to development; development adds life to momentum and accordingly, momentums lead to results. Such activities cannot be ad hoc; they have to be persistent in order to work. Discipline is the only thing known that can help to achieve this said consistency. Try any successful person and they will tell you that something must indeed be said about the lack of substitutes for discipline.

Your consistent mass actions should be enough, as it is recorded that once Dante said, the secret of getting things done is to act. And I will add that a formula behind undertaking actions is the inability to attempt doing everything great, to put one`s trust in little steps and little successes. Leave in your mind that good progress is good progress. The vision should be large, the project may be large, but each and every step can be dissected and the fact that baby steps are very important should never be underestimated.

Action and consistency would finally produce results; whenever in doubt of this principle, just refer to the stonecutter analogy. With this analogy, a stonecutter may strike and strike a rock with no apparent results. However, as it happens with the last stroke, right at that moment, the rock is chopped in two.

All you need is to remember that: in action, small things only, big things only, but never think that you stop. Failure is not an option. Whatever you do, you have to keep moving on, Martin Luther King said: If you can fly, do that; otherwise, run, then walk, crawl, but you should definitely have to keep going on.

## Flexible Routes

It is common to find people believing that once a plan has been made, then they are halfway there; now they only need to follow the plan and everything will work out. People with such thinking cannot be more wrong. Projects are fraught with so many instances in the pathway that will reinforce the lesson to you that you cannot simply be hard and just adhere to the plan. One of the best attributes of a leader is flexibility.

In handling your project, you should know how to take flexible routes.

## Adapt

When I was preparing a dissertation in my course of study, Human Resources Management, I realized that the most important trait in the current workforce is Adaptability. Recently, as Mike Koulianos described in an article in USF, Lifelong learning promotes adaptability. "Workforce adaptability emerges through education and training--

sometimes, by acquiring new, marketable skills and, at other times, by learning how to do familiar tasks in fresh ways."

Just like in the workforce, the capacity to adjust is pertinent in all factors of life and fundamental to the survival of mankind. As Mr. Koulianos told, it comes through continuous learning, which implies an understanding; it is through understanding, and accordingly, a mind that understands alone is flexible.

A good example of this is Nokia. They used to be the outright rulers of the cell phone business. They were well-set to have a solid product, plan and a colossal market share. However, they could not come in line with the changes when the market started to use smartphones. They were dogmatic, they adhered to the course of action, and their hitherto unconquerable empire fell. It is a painful yet valuable message; a strict outline is a path towards a path of failure. The plan is the territory.

**Resiliency**

The branches of the Tree of Success concept are resiliency, as I wrote in the book entitled Bajo la sombra del Exito in the Spanish version. This capacity to recover and restart, or as you also term it, the capacity to bounce back, is a very significant capacity in our trajectory to being very productive. It is easy to ask, in case you face any setbacks in achieving the results you do now, what will happen when you aspire to greater things? It is only natural that you will face increased failures. The weapon you will have to face that with is resiliency.

Not all challenges face us without failure and resiliency is not about being failure-free. It is about recovering when the event occurs. An obstacle is not a take-a-break sign; it is a detour sign. When any project goes awry, its most important team member quits, a technology is not working, a budget is reduced, a resilient leader does not say give up. They perceive it as a puzzle to solve. They pause to re-strategize, evaluate and then locate an alternative route to proceed.

What distinguishes between the winners and losers is the capacity to overcome an accident swiftly.

**Re-start**

It is said that, when the plan fails, change the plan but not the goal; this alteration of the plan usually entails restarting. In several instances, you may be forced to begin a new or a new project. The means to counter such kind of situations is to know not to equate new projects with poor performance in the past or even with the positive results in the past. With a worry of a different day and a different project, each project has its own troubles. The optimal is to know how to restart because comparison may be frustrating.

Failure is not a defeat; it is a trial in courage. Rarely is there anything better you can do than to discard a bad plan and begin again fresh. It is not enough, though, to just start over but instead, you need to start over with a different mindset. The container of previous failures cannot be loaded onto a new project. There is a lesson of the failure that you have to learn, but leave the emotion behind. Approach each new project differently, as a new problem, as a new opportunity. This kind of subtle art to confidently and smoothly hit the HIMt aggression reset button is not something that you should underestimate because it will save you invaluable amounts of time and dramatically spare you the frustration of immense proportions.

**The Project Manager's Mindset**

Outside of the concrete budget, schedule and scope skills, the most effective project managers have a particular attitude. They do not just wear the hats of the taskmasters but visionaries, problem-solvers and motivators. They can obtain an overview of the situation and, at the same time, grasp the minute details. They are used to doubt and can take decisive actions when pressure has occurred.

It is this mentality that enables a project manager to take the twists and turns that are an unpredictable process from idea to finished product. They are aware that no amount of planning can guarantee that projects will not present some kind of challenge. There is a plan, but there is the reality of a situation and a good project manager will manage that reality. They talk to their followers, inspire them and keep them on course towards the ultimate goal, even when the road becomes rocky.

Keep in mind that your life is the biggest project and you are its manager. These are not only business or career-enhancing skills you are studying in this book. They are to help you evolve; to make you happy; to make you live as you desire most. Therefore, learn these lessons and digest them in order to make the life you have always desired. The work has been started; it is turn to carry it to the end.

**The Power of the Team**

A project manager can only be as strong as his or her team. The greatest leaders understand that their role is not to complete all of the tasks per se rather to build an atmosphere in which the team should excel. This implies letting your team members be empowered, trusting them to get the job done and delegating decision-making to the team members. It is a paradigm change from a do-it-all attitude to a lead-the- way attitude. Your project management skills come to the surface through the way you delegate, as well as how you can form a cohesive team.

A group that is trusted and feels appreciated is more engaged, more creative, and more resilient. You will need to instill a culture of open communication where all team members will not hesitate to raise concerns, propose improvements, etc. and even confess mistakes without penalty. Keep in mind that a chain is as weak as its weakest link. The success of your project as an individual happens as a team effort; the role you have is to make sure that everyone is rowing in a similar direction, pursuing a common goal.

## The Art of Risk Management

Any project, in whichever magnitude, is accompanied by a certain degree of risk. This is the ambiguity we discussed in the making of decisions and this time we are going to encounter it head-on. An efficient project manager does not wish things to turn out well, but s/he prepares in case things go wrong. Risk management is dealing with the determination of possible issues and the evaluation of the probability and consequences of the issues in order to craft a strategy that prevents or minimizes their impact.

**Consider this analogy:** Assume that your project is the construction of a house, and the possible risk is the delay in an actor's supply chain of building materials. As a good project manager, you would pick up this risk rather early in the process, and your mitigation plan may be to source the materials from two different vendors or set aside a contingency fund to cover expedited shipping. This foresight and proactive planning could make the difference in a project, whether either succeeds or fails.

Risk management has four common strategies:

**Risk Avoidance:** Reformulating in order to avoid the risk altogether.

**Risk Mitigation:** Making efforts to lessen the probability or effects of the risk.

**Risk Transfer:** The act of transferring the risk to a third party, such as when one purchases insurance.

**Risk Acceptance:** Making a choice to take the risk and live with the consequences in case it happens.

Risks will surround project management decisions you will make and only how you handle them will lead you to success.

## The Importance of Closing the Loop

Other individuals are too stressed about meeting the project deadline to remember an important final stage, the close-out. Here, the closeout phase is where you officially complete the project. You deliver the final product, obtain sign-offs by all stakeholders and the most important of all, Post-Mortem Analysis.

A post-mortem analysis is a session during which you and your colleagues analyze what was positive, what was bad, or what could be done better on future projects. Here, you get to learn through the good and the bad. It is where you revise your standards, put into practice the battle rhythm, and further work on the decision-making process. An in-progress project that lacks a close-out is an opportunity lost to learning. The best individuals and organizations are those who never stop learning from their experiences.

This is the official spirit of the restart attitude. You end one project with a clear sense of what you have discovered, and have that discovery in the project you enter into next. This is like the difference between doing a project & project management.

Growth is the proof of progress. It is the invisible thread running through every discipline, every effort, and every challenge. While action sets things in motion, growth ensures that motion leads to transformation. Without growth, achievement is shallow and temporary. With growth, even small victories carry lasting significance.

Growth is layered. At the surface, it may look like new skills, better results, or outward success. But at its core, growth is an inward expansion, a broadening of vision, a deepening of resilience, and a refining of character. True growth makes you more capable not just of doing, but of enduring, leading, and influencing.

**Growth as Process, Not Event**

One of the most misunderstood aspects of growth is its nature. Growth does not happen in a single breakthrough moment. It is not one seminar, one book, or one victory that transforms you. Growth is gradual, cumulative, and often subtle. It happens day by day, through choices repeated, disciplines maintained, and lessons learned.

The seed analogy illustrates this truth. For weeks, nothing seems to happen after planting. The soil hides the progress, but below the surface, roots are spreading, preparing for the visible sprout. Many people give up too soon, failing to realize that growth often happens where eyes cannot see. The fruits of growth always appear later than the effort invested.

## The Cycles of Growth

Growth is rarely a straight, upward line. It comes in cycles, seasons of advancement, followed by seasons of testing or rest. The athlete grows stronger not just in training, but in recovery. The farmer gathers the harvest only after enduring long stretches of waiting. Similarly, personal growth includes times of momentum and times of stillness, both equally necessary. Setbacks, too, are part of this cycle. What feels like regression is often preparation. The project that fails teaches more than the project that succeeds. The challenge that breaks comfort builds resilience. Seen rightly, obstacles are not interruptions of growth but instruments of it.

## Growth and Identity

Perhaps the most powerful aspect of growth is its ability to reshape identity. It transforms how you see yourself. Where you once identified with limitations, you now recognize capacity. The timid person discovers courage, the undisciplined finds structure, and the doubter develops confidence. Growth rewrites the story you tell yourself.

This identity shift is crucial because sustainable change flows from who you believe yourself to be. When you see yourself as someone capable of learning, enduring, and succeeding, your actions follow naturally. Identity fuels behavior, and growth refines identity.

## The Demands of Growth

Growth is not effortless. It requires tension, struggle, and stretching. Comfort zones must be left behind. Familiar patterns must be questioned. Growth demands humility, the acknowledgment that you have more to learn and courage, the willingness to step into the unfamiliar.

It also requires patience. Just as no child becomes an adult overnight, no one grows in maturity, skill, or influence without time. Those who demand instant results often quit too early. Those who understand growth as a lifelong process remain steady, trusting that persistence yields compound returns.

## Growth Beyond the Self

True growth extends beyond personal achievement. As you expand, you gain the ability to lift others. Your progress creates pathways for those who follow. Your wisdom shortens their learning curve. Your character provides an example. Growth is not hoarded; it is multiplied through influence.

In this way, growth creates a ripple effect. The lessons you learn become the legacy you leave. The impact is not just measured by what you accomplish, but by who is transformed because you chose to grow.

## Becoming More

Ultimately, growth is not about getting more; it is about becoming more. More aware, more resilient, more skillful, more compassionate. Success may add to your life, but growth enlarges your life. It ensures that each challenge faced, each victory won, and each lesson learned shape you into someone stronger, wiser, and more capable than before.

Growth is both the reward of effort and the preparation for greater effort ahead. It is never final, never finished. The journey of growth is the journey of a lifetime.

## Reflection

Looking back on wins and losses, analyzing what worked, and identifying lessons to carry forward. Growth is more than the act of moving forward; it is also the discipline of looking backward. Action without reflection can create motion without meaning, progress without direction. Reflection is the process of pausing to examine where you have been, what you have done, and what it has taught you. It is in this quiet pause that lessons emerge, turning experiences into wisdom and setbacks into stepping stones.

Without reflection, victories are forgotten too quickly, and failures repeat themselves. With it, nothing is wasted.

## The Meaning of Looking Back

Looking back is not nostalgia, and it is not regret. It is a purposeful review. Every victory carries seeds of insight, signs of preparation, persistence, creativity, or teamwork that led to success. To reflect is to identify those seeds, so they can be planted again. Every loss, on the other hand, leaves behind traces of why it occurred, distractions, poor planning, lack of focus, or hesitation. To reflect is to uncover these traces and learn from them, so the same mistakes do not resurface.

When you reflect, you grow twice: once through the experience itself, and again through the wisdom you extract from it.

## Reflection as a Tool for Growth

Not everyone grows through experience. Some people repeat the same mistakes year after year because they never take the time to examine them. Reflection is what transforms a simple experience into deep growth. It multiplies the value of everything you go through.

Two people can encounter the same obstacle. One walks away bitter and unchanged, blaming the situation. The other takes time to reflect, asks what could have been done differently, accepts responsibility, and adapts. The same circumstance produced two very different outcomes. The difference was not in the event, it was in the reflection.

## The Courage of Honest Evaluation

Reflection demands courage. It is easy to look back on wins and celebrate them, but harder to face failures with honesty. It asks uncomfortable questions: *Where did I fall short? Where did I let fear or laziness guide me? What did I avoid because it was difficult?* Facing these truths can sting, but it is also freeing. When you stop hiding from the reality of your choices, you reclaim the power to change them.

Honest reflection is not about guilt or shame; it is about clarity. Without clarity, change is impossible. With clarity, growth becomes inevitable.

## Creating Time and Space for Reflection

The pace of modern life makes reflection difficult. We are conditioned to value constant motion, to move from one task to the next without pause. But without time to reflect, experiences pass through us without leaving wisdom behind. Growth requires intentional space.

Reflection can take many forms. For some, it is the daily discipline of journaling. For others, it is quiet solitude, a morning walk, or prayer. It may come through reviewing key moments of the week, or through conversations with trusted mentors. The form matters less than the intention. What matters is carving out the margin to stop, think, and learn.

**Turning Lessons into Action**

Reflection without application is incomplete. Insights must become actions, or they will fade quickly. It is not enough to know what worked or what failed; you must integrate those lessons into the way you live, work, and lead.

One way to anchor reflection is by recording lessons in a permanent way, through journals, notes, or digital tools. Over time, this collection becomes a personal library of wisdom, a map of progress. Each time you face a new challenge, you are not starting from scratch; you are guided by the accumulated wisdom of your own journey.

**Reflection and Gratitude**

Reflection is not just about analyzing; it is also about appreciating. Looking back allows you to see not only what went wrong but also how much has gone right. It highlights progress you may have overlooked, showing you how far you have come compared to where you started. It reveals how challenges shaped you, how people supported you, and how perseverance carried you through. Gratitude turns reflection into a source of strength, keeping you grounded in humility while fueling confidence for the road ahead.

## The Bridge Between Past and Future

Ultimately, reflection is the bridge between past experience and future growth. It ensures that nothing is wasted, not the victories, not the failures, not even the quiet seasons of waiting. Each moment, when reflected on, becomes part of a larger pattern, shaping you into someone wiser, stronger, and more resilient.

Without reflection, you risk running in circles, repeating old mistakes, and missing opportunities for improvement. With reflection, every season whether filled with triumph or trial, becomes part of your transformation. Reflection does not trap you in the past; it equips you for the future. It allows you to live with clarity, move with wisdom, and grow with intention.

## Scaling Up

Expanding efforts, leveraging systems, and multiplying results without losing quality. Scaling up is the turning point where effort transforms into legacy. It is the stage where your vision begins to stretch beyond your personal capacity, demanding more than hard work alone. While beginnings are often carried by sheer determination, late nights, persistence, and a willingness to do whatever it takes, scaling up requires something different. It requires wisdom. It requires foresight. It requires the courage to let go of control so that growth can multiply without collapsing under its own weight.

At its core, scaling is not about doing more; it is about doing differently. It is about moving from dependence on the individual to reliance on systems, structures, and shared ownership. Without scaling, growth eventually stalls, capped by personal limits. With scaling, the same vision can reach further, touch more lives, and endure for longer than one person's strength ever could.

## From Effort to Architecture

At the beginning, progress comes from energy. You move forward because you are willing to push harder than others, to grind when others rest. But effort alone is fragile; it cannot sustain limitless growth. Scaling requires architecture. It is the deliberate construction of processes, workflows, and patterns that allow excellence to repeat itself without needing constant reinvention.

Architecture is what separates temporary hustle from lasting growth. Just as a building cannot rise without blueprints, expansion cannot endure without design. Scaling up asks you to step back from the busyness of doing to the discipline of building.

## Multiplication Through People

Systems are powerful, but they are not enough. Scaling requires people. The greater the vision, the greater the need for hands, minds, and hearts to carry it forward. No orchard thrives because of one gardener alone; it thrives because many tenders work together, each caring for the trees, each protecting the soil, each ensuring the harvest.

Delegation in scaling is not about offloading what you do not want to do, it is about empowerment. It is entrusting others not just with responsibility but with ownership. When you teach, train, and transfer values as well as tasks, you do not merely multiply labor; you multiply leadership. This is how scaling transforms from fragile growth into sustainable expansion.

## Guarding Against Dilution

The greatest danger of scaling is dilution. In the rush to expand, quality can slip, values can blur, and the essence that made success possible can disappear. Scaling without standards is like pouring water into wine; it may create more volume, but it weakens the strength.

True scaling preserves the essence while expanding the reach. It means defining what must never be compromised, quality, integrity, service, and embedding those values into every system and every person involved. Growth is not just about spreading out; it is about spreading strong.

## The Mindset Shift

Scaling demands a new way of thinking. On a small scale, the mindset is often survival: *What must I do to make this work today?* But at scale, the mindset shifts to sustainability: *How can this continue to work tomorrow, next year, and long after I am gone?*

This requires letting go of perfectionism and micromanagement. It means resisting the urge to hold everything in your own hands and instead trusting the systems and people you have built. Scaling is as much about humility as it is about vision, the humility to recognize that others can carry the mission as well as, or even better than, you can.

## Nature's Lesson: The Orchard vs. the Tree

A single tree can grow tall and produce fruit, but its harvest is limited. If you tend only one tree, you feed a few. But if you plant an orchard, designing for growth, preparing the soil, and multiplying trees, you create abundance that can feed generations. Scaling up is the move from tree to orchard. It is the deliberate decision to multiply what works so that its impact is not limited to your strength or lifespan.

This is why scaling matters: it transforms temporary success into generational significance.

## Expanding Influence, Extending Legacy

Scaling is not only about size; it is about influence. A vision that scales, reaches people you may never meet, solves problems you may never see, and creates ripples far beyond your immediate reach. It allows your work to move from being an individual achievement to a collective force.

Without scaling, your progress ends when your effort ends. With scaling, your progress continues even when you step back. It becomes bigger than you, strong enough to survive without your constant presence, resilient enough to grow even when you are no longer there to guide it.

Scaling up, then, is not just a strategy for growth; it is an act of legacy. It is the deliberate choice to build something that lasts, something that multiplies, something that continues to impact long after the first builder has stepped away.

## The Weight of Scaling Well

Scaling requires discipline. It requires letting go of ego, resisting shortcuts, and guarding against complacency. It is tempting to think growth alone is enough, but poor scaling can collapse faster than no growth at all. The challenge is not to expand quickly, but to expand wisely.

Done well, scaling creates stability. Done poorly, it creates fragility. That is why scaling is not a one-time achievement but a continual process of refinement, learning, and strengthening.

Scaling up is not the end of growth; it is the deepening of it. It is the point where success ceases to be measured only by what you can do and begins to be measured by what you can build. It is the art of multiplying without weakening, expanding without losing focus, and leaving behind more than what you alone could accomplish.

Scaling up is where success turns into significance, and where personal achievement transforms into enduring impact.

## Legacy

Building habits and structures that last, leaving behind value for yourself, your team, and others. Legacy is the ultimate expression of growth. It is the evidence that your work, your choices, and your character did not fade with time but continued to shape lives beyond your direct influence. Legacy is not a single act, nor is it created at the end of life, it is built day by day, in the habits you practice, the systems you establish, and the values you embody. It is the sum of small, consistent actions that echo far beyond the moment.

Many chase success, but few think about legacy. Success asks, *what can I achieve?* Legacy asks, *What will remain when I am gone?* Success is about climbing the mountain; legacy is about leaving a trail others can follow.

**The Foundation of Habits**

Habits form the bedrock of legacy. What you consistently practice becomes the story others remember you by. A single achievement can inspire admiration, but repeated integrity builds trust that lasts. A single act of kindness may brighten a day, but a life patterned with compassion changes entire communities.

Legacy does not emerge from occasional bursts of greatness; it emerges from the steady rhythm of discipline. Each decision to act with integrity, each moment of perseverance in difficulty, each choice to prioritize growth over comfort plants seeds that take root in the lives of others.

## Structures That Outlast the Builder

Beyond habits lies structure. A legacy built only on personality risks vanishing when the person is gone. But a legacy rooted in systems, standards, and culture creates permanence. Structures serve as anchors, ensuring that excellence, accountability, and purpose endure even when leadership changes hands.

Consider the great institutions of history, schools, hospitals, movements, that long outlived their founders. Their endurance was not an accident; it was the result of values embedded into systems that could be passed down, protected, and expanded. This is the power of structure: it makes legacy transferable.

## The Power of Influence

At the heart of every legacy lies people. Buildings may crumble, systems may evolve, but people carry values forward. Each person you mentor, train, or inspire becomes a living extension of your impact. Influence multiplies when it is shared.

This is why legacy thrives not in control but in empowerment. True legacy is not about binding people to your way of doing things, it is about equipping them with principles they can adapt and carry into new situations.

When you give people tools and trust, you extend your reach into places you will never step, into futures you will never see.

## Legacy vs. Recognition

A common mistake is to confuse legacy with recognition. Fame fades; legacy endures. Recognition is about being remembered; legacy is about what is remembered. A name may be forgotten, but the influence of a life well-lived can ripple for generations.

A teacher may not be remembered by name decades later, yet their lessons shape the lives of students who, in turn, shape others. A parent's sacrifices may go uncelebrated, but their character shapes the next generation. Legacy is not about being visible, it is about being valuable.

## Living Legacy in the Present

Legacy is not something you leave behind only at the end of your life, it is something you live now. Every interaction, every project, every decision contributes to the story others will tell. To live with legacy in mind is to act with the awareness that your choices are not isolated but part of a greater narrative.

Living legacy means asking: *Does this decision align with my values? Am I building something that will last, or something that will fade? Will this benefit only me, or will it strengthen others too?* When these questions guide your choices, legacy becomes less about chance and more about intention.

## Seeds and Forests

Legacy is like planting seeds. A seed is small, unimpressive, even fragile, but when planted with care, it can grow into a tree that provides shade, fruit, and shelter long after the planter is gone. And when many seeds are planted, a forest emerges, a living, breathing testament to foresight and care.

Your actions today are seeds. Some may sprout quickly, others may take years, but all carry the potential to outlast you. The question is not whether you are planting, because every choice plants something, the question is what kind of forest you are cultivating.

## The True Measure of Legacy

The true measure of legacy is not wealth, titles, or applause. It is the values you leave, the people you influence, and the systems you build that outlast your presence. Legacy is the assurance that your life mattered, not because of what you gained, but because of what you gave. It is not the loudest lives that leave the deepest mark, but the most consistent ones. The quiet father who worked faithfully, the leader who prioritized integrity over profit, the friend who gave selflessly, these create legacies as enduring as any empire.

Legacy is not an accident. It is the deliberate work of building habits that inspire, structures that endure, and lives that ripple outward. It is the transformation of personal growth into communal inheritance, the shift from *me* to *we*, from *today* to *tomorrow.*

And in the end, legacy is the truest test of growth, not what you achieved for yourself, but what you set in motion for others.

## Final Thoughts on a Lifetime of Projects

Life itself is a project and is all about projects, budgets, schedules, and scopes. Your schooling was an undertaking. Your first work was a project. Meeting somebody, getting married, and making a career are tremendous projects on which you, as a project manager, are engaged.

These principles, written in this chapter, of making bold choices, taking deliberate actions, being adaptive, and risk management, are not only confined to the workplace scenario. They are the secrets to a well-managed life. Time, after all, is your most valuable commodity, and you know, your own life is the project that you will never regret working on. Therefore, do it consciously, do it attentively, and with the will to change something. The thing is, your desired results are waiting. The time has come to get to work.

# Section II. The Tools

At this moment, you have in your head, notes and hands the three most crucial skills you require in order to increase your productivity. That is the right moment to put your toolbox into preparing yourself to succeed. In this part, I will present you with three tools that will enable you to increase your output on the same resources.

The same results will enable you to be more productive in your work by increasing your productivity. This commitment entailed nine concepts; the tools are the second and third of this scheme. It is time we found out what tools we need to win the desired results.

# Chapter Four: The Checklist

Several years into my professional life, I realized that a pen, a notepad and a highlighter can be a powerful tool indeed. When I was in the military, these three items were even items of inspection. Today, I can share with you that these are the things that made me acquainted with the powerful checklist.

When the entire team works according to a list of executions, individual goals, as well as organizational goals, are not missed. The most effective contribution to productivity is to set goals and once you know your goals, you break them down. A checklist is the written description of all the activities that should be completed to attain a goal. The goals now have a clear picture of what must be done in the course of the day, week, or month.

It is the effectiveness of a checklist that makes it so accurate that you will use it to its full extent. You need it at the formulation of your goals, in the planning period and definitely when you are out there in action, headed towards the finishing line. A properly drawn checklist will guide you not only to have a November planning but also to learn to use time more efficiently. When defining checklists to squeeze most of your time resources, the basic sections should at least be covered. On the lower end of the spectrum, your checklist should at least have

- **Title:** It gives the checklist a relevant feel. You cannot come up with a list containing various tasks that are not relevant to one another. The title will ensure that all work remains in the same objective and at the same stage.
- **Date:** Put the date on which you are writing the list. You can add this date later with the task timelines, so you can have accurate information on how you used the time.
- **Tasks/Subtask:** This is merely a description of the task to be performed and implied tasks that will need to be done in order to complete the main task.
- **Timelines:** In this column, add the due date that you want to have the work accomplished.
- **Remarks:** This column will be used to make any notes, inconveniences, as well as miscellaneous items that occur during the completion of the task.

There are individuals who say that the process is the most important part of the entire objective. They claim to enjoy the process, learn through the process, bla bla. I can go slightly further and say that one, be very observant of the process, as it is in the process where the productivity can increase, and in the process where results are put to the test. Why is the relevance of the checklist to this?

It is due to the fact that the process has to be cross-referred to the checklist and to the standards.

**The Psychology of the Checklist**

Have you ever wondered why it feels so good to start scratching off an item on a list? It is a mental phenomenon. Every time you finish a task, there is a release of a little bit of dopamine, which is the neurotransmitter that we associate with pleasure and motivation. This has a positive feedback cycle effect. As soon as you cross out certain jobs on the list, you feel more motivated, and this helps you to do another task. A list of things to do does not, on its own, encourage you to continue, but rather is a checklist that has a definite visual representation of what you have already done. It is evidence of the fact that you are progressing.

What is most amazing about the checklist is that it is simple. It divides cumbersome, frightening programs into a sequence of smaller, doable ones. Such as example, the set mission--Write a book may be intimidating. However, in breakdown form, the checklist idea, like "Outline Chapter 1," "Write first draft of Chapter 1," and so on, the idea, along with the end paragraph, gets very close. This is how you make a vision a reality

## Beyond the Basics: Advanced Checklist Strategies

As much as a checklist can be effective, you can utilize it at a higher level:

- **Prioritization:** Do not compile tasks in a random manner. You can use something like the Eisenhower Matrix (Urgent/ Important) or label tasks A, B and C to indicate their priorities. This keeps you on track, doing what is important all the time.

- **Delegation:** A checklist does not include you alone. If you head a team, a checklist will help you to delegate responsibilities to others. The checklist is an agreed point of truth, so there is no ambiguity, and assistance with accountability.

- **Routine Checklists:** Develop a routine checklist that covers your daily, weekly and monthly routines. This can be such things as your daily morning routine ("Make bed," "Meditate," "Review top 3 tasks") as well as a process that you engage in at the end of the week ("Empty inbox," "Plan for next week," "Review financial goals"). These checklists take your habits out of the equation and leave your mind to concentrate on tougher decisions.

A checklist is your battle plan, your roadmap and a document to show progress all rolled in one. It is a humble instrument and yet in the possession of a well-trained, conscientious person, it can be a formidable mechanism. Don't go home without it.

# Chapter Five: Standards operating procedures (SOP)

By now, we are halfway into the book of productivity and we get into the meat of any operation. These documents give the best insight into a company like an X-ray. Reading the Standard Operating Procedure of any firm, you will be able to comprehend and analyze its processes in no time. We have discussed time usage briefly and now it is time to get in- depth on part of one of the most important aspects of a company SOP.

Have you ever wondered how such multinational corporations as Amazon, McDonald's, or Nike are able to extend their activities around the world and preserve their quality and individuality? That is the Standards Operating Procedures. These firms operate their operations involving the bare minimum and strictly imposed rules. Do you like McDonald's fries, e.g.? Understanding that worldwide their fries are liked indiscriminately, I can say to you that as soon as you get to like their fries in the USA, you will also like them in South Korea. Their process of making French fries is identical the world over, starting with the temperature of their oil up through to even how many times you shake with the salt.

SOPs may be time-consuming to effectively develop and implement, but trust me, it is worth more than gold. As soon as one has a clear vision of the purpose where s/he want to move and what to accomplish, it is easy to make standards. Here are three areas to bear in mind during the establishment of standards or the development of SOPs.

## The Foundation of Consistency

SOPs are the DNA of an organization. They capture the knowledge and best practices of a team and formalize them into an executable process. SOPs will continually save you the time of reinventing the wheel. A new worker wouldn't be trained to go up and down the ladder, errors would be repeated and the quality of your work could not be predicted. Using a properly documented SOP, you establish a foundation of best practice. Everyone knows precisely what, how and the reason why it is done in such a way. This saves time, minimizes some errors and makes the success of a project not rest on the individual executing the task.

On your personal projects, an SOP may appear to be a matter of inessentiality, but it is a life-changer. Is there a process in the way you write? What is your money style? How do you do a once-a-week review?

Putting these workflows into your own personal SOP will greatly increase your efficiency and lessen the impact of wrestling with the question of what to do next.

## How the SOP Should Be Written

- **Concise:** There must be no grounds for misunderstanding. Write using simple language and keep away from jargon. Each step should be explained in the most comprehensible manner that fits anybody, whether a beginner or an advanced one.

- **Short:** A long-winded SOP will not be deployed. Make it as brief as it can be with only the crucial steps. Please subdivide a process that is too complex to follow into more than one SOP.

- **Simple:** The style must be easy to comprehend. Use bullet points, and numbered lists and bold headings so the document can be scanned.

## The Basic Components

- **Administrative:** The administrative segment of the SOP may comprise the title of SOP, the name of the person who wrote it, and the date of its approval. This injects some form of formality and aids in version control.

- **Generals:** The general details of the SOP will come after the admin details and will comprise of purpose, scope, responsibilities, sources used, timelines and frequently asked questions. The section provides the necessary context and makes everybody aware of the whys of the process.

This part is where a details step-by-step description of procedures to be carried out is provided. This is the essence of the SOP, the step-by-step instructions on how to go through the process.

**Steps to Create an SOP**

- **Identify:** to determine a clear need for the necessary use and creation of an SOP. Why is this process documented? What are the recurrent/inefficiencies/problems that an SOP can address?

- **Plan:** Begin planning out the SOP by breaking the process into the smallest steps. Now it is time to apply your checklist skills as you record every single thing that needs to happen.

- **Review:** Have the staff who will be working in the course of implementing the procedure review the SOP. The worst thing you want to do is to attempt to stamp some kind of standard that makes absolutely no sense, or, lacking sense, is somehow completely irrelevant to the people who are going to be using it. This feedback cycle is vital in making sure that the SOP is workable and viable.

- **Training:** Talk and allocate duties to various activities. Train the individuals who will have to accomplish the particular task in the process and have them understand. You cannot, by handing a person an SOP, give them an option to follow it by the book. It is imperative that training is done properly.

- **Review 2:** Once again, we are creatures of habits, so bear in mind that, as with everything, you must maintain balance. With these standards, we develop habits and with these habits, there lies the risk of falling into the comfort zone. To prevent it, the SOP that is implemented should be examined subsequently. Depending on the frequency with which you carry out these processes, define a regular review every now and then to check on relevancy and accuracy.

**Benefits of the SOPs**

- **Removal of the Clutter:** All are familiar with what is expected.
- **Give Consistency:** The outcome/product is always the same.
- **You can responsibly Project Results:** With a greater level of precision, you can predict results.
- **Safety:** it makes you and your staff safer against mistakes.

SOPs are the mainstay of any operation, whether large or small. They are the background actors that make a project go well, a business remain in good standing and a team move in the right direction. Your adherence to the establishment and adherence to them is a direct contribution to your future success.

# Chapter Six: Key Performance Indicators (KPI)

Remind yourself of S.M.A.R.T. A specific the measurable portion of that concept is what we will develop further in this tool. Success is a numbers game and whoever stated it first was a genius. In order to monitor a group or individual goal, you will need to measure as much as possible. It is at this point that Key Performance Indicators come in.

In case you have anything like me and like numbers, you would find KPIs. KPIs are not greater than excellent parts of the operation that can be evaluated on a regular basis to validate the correctness, relevance and improvement. They assist in the formulation of strategies and growth in operations.

Put it this way, you have a clear vision and a distinct plan, now you can create the KPIs along with every task in the process.

With the availability of numerous software and analytic platforms these modern days, it is quite an easy task to monitor and report on KPIs. A business should have no reason to fail when it comes to determining the most important indicators and evaluating its performance to monitor and work out strategies.

**Why You Can't Manage What You Can't Measure**

This is the central ideology of KPIs. Once you are without data, you fly blind. You may think that you are improving, but is it true or just a feeling? KPIs supply the objective truth. They will be straightforward in telling you whether you are within range, behind, or surpassing expectations. They eliminate the guesswork in productivity and replace it with a clear, data-driven roadmap.

As an example, you may wish to lose weight. Without KPI, this objective is in vain. How will you know that you are succeeding? The KPI makes this more tangible and measurable, such as: "Lose 10 pounds within 60 days." Through this, you now have a number to track. You could weigh yourself on a weekly basis, and in case you are not meeting your targets, you can revise your action plan by altering your diet or ramping up your exercise. That is the KPIs' power at work.

**Types of KPIs**

- **Operational:** Operational KPIs concentrate on shorter time intervals as short as the day-to-day operation. An operational performance indicator may include such an example as the fulfillment time of orders when selling an online product.

- **Functional:** These KPIs are committed to a section/department of an organization. The finance department of a company will have good examples, such as the data of Return on Investment, financial level of profits, budget compliance, cash flow reliability, etc.

- **Historical:** All of your past data will be viewed as historical KPI. These lessons learned or historical data will help you design new or revise your SOPs.

- **Strategic:** Strategic KPIs look at the orchestration of company operations. These are more goal-oriented.

Collectively, Key Performance Indicators aid a firm and individuals to make informed decisions, enhance performance, hold team members accountable and enhance communication. In Synopsis, there is no downside to identifying the elements in my operation to measure, track and report on the progress.

**How to Create Powerful KPIs**

Developing a KPI is more than selecting a figure. It is the right questions that one should ask. Decision-maker needs to know what he/she wants to achieve prior to selecting a KPI and what information is most prized to him/her.

- **Clearness of objectives:** Objectives run on clarity, especially when determining your performance indicators. Achievable goals are typically what dictate effective KPI. The best way to drive clarity towards your objectives will require that you ask Key Performance Questions, where the answers will help you select appropriate KPIs.

- **Adaptability:** The identification is only part of the KPI activity; they are not ordinary indicators, but key indicators. We are operating in a highly dynamic environment and the KPIs and flexibility go hand in hand and they should be dynamic to work well.

- **Light levels:** Don't underrate the power of baby steps. Every step is a step in the right direction; when you keep the increment level of progress lower, you can monitor them more frequently and gauge improvement. When measured against KPIs, small improvements may reveal trends, suggest techniques that are working, and warn of what may be cutting across the grain.

The most widespread error that people make is that they select too many KPIs. This results in analysis paralysis- by spending all your time counting and none of your time doing. A few carefully selected KPIs are much more potent than a dozen useless ones.

**The Feedback Loop**

Checklists are related to SOPs and KPIs that offer a strong feedback mechanism. You apply your checklist in performing your daily routine. Your SOPs make such tasks consistent in terms of quality. Your KPIs quantify the outcomes of what you are doing and give you the information you need to determine whether your processes are effective. When you see no progress, you track back on your SOPs to determine whether there is an inefficient step or an outdated step. Assuming your SOP is in good shape, you might need to change what you are taking down on the checklist.

This Checklist/SOP/KPI trifecta is a complete project management toolkit, and can be applied across the board, whether by a multinational CEO or a regular person attempting to do more in their daily life. You use simple tools, but it takes discipline, desire to learn and commitment to improving to apply them. With these tools in your hands, you are no longer envisioning success; you are creating a system that will make success inevitable.

Action is the bridge between where you are and where you want to be. The first three sections, *The Skills, The Tools, and The Laws*, have equipped you with clarity, structure, and principles. But knowledge without action is wasted potential. This section is about taking decisive steps, creating momentum, and ensuring that what you know becomes part of what you *do*.

True achievement doesn't come from grand intentions; it comes from consistent execution. Many people plan but never follow through. Others start with energy but lose focus when challenges arise. To move past these obstacles, you need to build a rhythm of implementation, stay adaptable in the face of change, and pursue excellence in execution.

In this section, you will learn:

- **Implementation**: how to turn goals into practical, manageable actions and develop habits that lead to steady progress.

- **Adaptability**: how to remain flexible, adjust your methods when circumstances shift, and keep moving forward despite setbacks.

- **Execution Excellence**: how to hold yourself to a higher standard, measure outcomes, and constantly refine your performance for lasting results.

## Implementation

Implementation is the engine of progress. Without it, even the most inspiring ideas remain untested, and the most carefully crafted plans gather dust. Implementation is the practice of turning thought into action, of bridging the gap between "what could be" and "what is." It demands clarity, discipline, and above all, consistency.

## From Vision to Action

The first step of implementation is translation, breaking big goals into actionable steps. Dreams and visions are often too large to act on directly. They must be translated into small, specific behaviors that can be performed today. For example, "write a book" becomes "write 500 words every morning," and "get healthier" becomes "replace soda with water this week." When you learn to reduce lofty goals into daily actions, you make the path to achievement not only clear but manageable.

## The Power of Starting Small

Grand ambitions can be paralyzing. People often fail not because their goals are too high, but because their first step is too big. Implementation requires the wisdom to start small. A small action may feel insignificant in the moment, but repeated consistently, it builds momentum. That momentum creates confidence, and confidence fuels larger steps. Small beginnings prevent overwhelm, reduce procrastination, and transform intentions into tangible results.

## Building Consistency: The Compounding Effect

Implementation succeeds when actions become habits. Consistency is the multiplier of effort. It is better to act consistently in small ways than to act sporadically in large ones. Just as water shapes stone through steady dripping, consistency shapes success through repeated effort.

Creating consistency often requires systems: routines, schedules, accountability partners, or reminders. These systems reduce reliance on willpower by making action automatic. Over time, consistent habits compound like interest, creating results far beyond what irregular bursts of effort could achieve.

## Feedback and Adjustment

Implementation is not a rigid process; it is a learning loop. Each action produces a result, and that result provides feedback. Tracking progress helps you see what is working and what is not. With feedback, you refine your methods, improve efficiency, and eliminate wasteful effort.

This cycle, act, measure, and adjust is the backbone of effective implementation. Without it, you risk repeating ineffective actions. With it, you become agile, steadily moving closer to your goal through deliberate improvement.

## Imperfect Action Over Perfect Plans

A common barrier to implementation is the desire for perfection. Many people delay action, waiting for the "perfect time" or the "perfect plan." But perfection is an illusion, and waiting only stalls progress. Imperfect beats perfect inaction. By starting where you are, with what you have, you gain real-world experience. Mistakes become lessons, and lessons accelerate growth.

## Sustaining Momentum

The final key to implementation is sustainability. Bursts of enthusiasm are easy; endurance is rare. To sustain momentum, you must protect your energy, pace yourself, and celebrate progress along the way. Small rewards for small wins reinforce motivation and remind you that growth is happening, even if it feels slow.

Implementation, then, is not a single decision but a daily commitment. It is the discipline of reducing dreams into steps, taking those steps consistently, learning from feedback, and refusing to wait for perfection. Knowledge may light the path, but only implementation carries you down it. Every action, no matter how small, is a brick in the foundation of success.

## Adaptability

Adaptability is the ability to adjust without losing direction, to bend without breaking, and to evolve without abandoning your core values. It is the trait that turns uncertainty into opportunity and transforms challenges into stepping stones. Where knowledge gives you clarity and implementation gets you started, adaptability ensures you stay on course even when the terrain shifts beneath your feet.

## The Reality of Change

One truth you cannot escape is that change is constant. Technology advances, economies rise and fall, industries reinvent themselves, and life circumstances shift, often without warning. If you build your success on the assumption that conditions will remain the same, you set yourself up for disappointment. Those who thrive are not the ones who cling to stability but those who expect change and prepare to navigate it.

Think of a tree in a storm. The rigid tree, unwilling to bend, risks snapping under pressure. The flexible tree, however, sways with the wind and survives. Adaptability is that flexibility; it does not weaken you, it preserves you.

## Anchored in Vision

Being adaptable does not mean drifting aimlessly, changing direction with every obstacle. Adaptability must always be anchored to a clear long-term vision. Your vision is the compass, the "why" behind everything you do. The adaptable person understands that while the *destination* remains fixed, the *route* may change many times.

A sailor embodies this principle. The wind may shift suddenly, but instead of abandoning the journey, the sailor adjusts the sails. The ship stays on course, not by resisting the wind, but by cooperating with it. Adaptability is the skill applied to life and work, adjusting the sails without losing sight of the horizon.

## Resilience in Setbacks

Adaptability requires resilience, the capacity to recover quickly from failure, disappointment, or loss. Plans fail, projects stall, relationships shift, and unexpected crises arise. The rigid person sees setbacks as defeat; the adaptable person views them as feedback. Instead of asking *"Why did this happen to me?"* they ask, *"What can I learn, and how do I move forward?"*

Resilience doesn't mean ignoring pain or frustration. It means refusing to let those emotions paralyze you. You acknowledge the difficulty, but then you rise again with new insight. Every setback becomes a teacher, and every adjustment makes you stronger.

## Learning Agility

A core dimension of adaptability is learning agility, the willingness to acquire new skills, perspectives, and strategies in response to change. What worked yesterday may not work tomorrow. Adaptable people embrace lifelong learning as a survival skill.

This may mean upgrading your technical skills in a rapidly evolving industry, learning cultural sensitivity in a globalized workplace, or developing emotional intelligence when leading diverse teams. Adaptability is fueled by curiosity and humility, the recognition that you don't know everything, but you can learn.

## Emotional Flexibility

Adaptability is not only strategic, it is emotional. Change often brings fear, frustration, or uncertainty. If unchecked, these emotions cloud judgment and trigger impulsive reactions. Emotional flexibility is the ability to regulate your feelings, maintain perspective, and respond thoughtfully rather than react blindly.

Adaptable people do not deny their emotions; they acknowledge them without letting them take control. They cultivate calm in chaos, which allows them to see clearly when others panic. This emotional steadiness is a superpower in moments of disruption.

## Turning Setbacks into Opportunities

The hallmark of adaptability is the ability to turn obstacles into opportunities. A canceled plan may free time for reflection. A failed product may spark innovation. A career setback may redirect you toward a path that fits you better. Where others see endings, adaptable people see beginnings.

History is full of examples: companies that reinvented themselves when industries shifted, leaders who changed strategies during crises, and individuals who used personal setbacks to grow stronger. Adaptability transforms adversity into advantage by asking, *"How can I use this?"* rather than

*"Why me?"*

## The Core Principle

In essence, adaptability is being firm in your goals but flexible in your methods. It means holding tightly to your vision while being willing to release old strategies when they no longer serve you. Those who master adaptability don't just survive change; they grow because of it.

Adaptability is not a weakness; it is a strength. It is the ability to remain rooted while bending, to embrace uncertainty without losing purpose, and to continually evolve in pursuit of your highest goals. In a world where certainty is rare, adaptability is the one constant advantage you can cultivate.

## Execution Excellence

Maintaining discipline, tracking progress, and striving for continuous improvement in every task. Execution is the great equalizer. Ideas may inspire, strategies may organize, and goals may motivate, but without strong execution, none of them produce results. Execution is where preparation meets reality, where intentions transform into outcomes. Excellence in execution elevates ordinary work into extraordinary achievement. It is the discipline of doing things not just quickly or sufficiently, but with precision, consistency, and pride.

## Discipline: The Foundation of Excellence

The cornerstone of execution is discipline. Discipline is the ability to act according to values and commitments rather than moods or circumstances. It is doing what must be done, even on the days when motivation is absent. Many people are talented. Many have vision. But talent without discipline produces inconsistency, and vision without discipline remains a dream.

Excellence requires showing up daily with intention. Like an athlete who trains consistently, not just when it feels convenient, disciplined individuals build habits that compound into mastery. It is better to progress an inch every day than to surge forward in bursts and collapse in exhaustion. The disciplined executor understands that steady progress always outlasts sporadic effort.

## Tracking Progress: Turning Effort into Data

Execution is not blind action; it is guided action. What gets measured gets improved, and what goes unmeasured often fades into neglect. Tracking progress provides the clarity needed to distinguish between movement and true advancement.

Systems of measurement may vary, key performance indicators in business, journals or trackers in personal development, or feedback loops in team projects. The purpose is always the same: to create visibility. When progress is visible, it fuels motivation. Each small milestone becomes proof of movement, and each data point becomes a guide for refinement. Without tracking, people confuse activity with productivity. With tracking, every action is evaluated for impact.

**Continuous Improvement: Raising the Standard**

Execution excellence is not a single achievement; it is a commitment to continuous improvement. Those who excel are never content with "good enough." They constantly ask, *"What can I refine? What can I improve? How can this be done better?"*

This pursuit of refinement is what creates breakthroughs. It is the mindset behind every advancement in technology, art, business, and personal growth. Small improvements, repeated consistently, compound into transformation. Yet, continuous improvement demands humility. To improve, one must admit imperfection. It requires curiosity, the willingness to experiment, and the courage to seek feedback even when it is uncomfortable. The person committed to improvement understands that mastery is not a destination but an evolving process.

## Quality Over Speed: Excellence is Sustainable

In a world obsessed with speed, execution excellence values quality over haste. Fast work can deliver quick results, but it often sacrifices depth, accuracy, or sustainability. Excellence, by contrast, is thorough, intentional, and enduring.

This does not mean excellence is slow; it means it is deliberate. It balances efficiency with attention to detail, ensuring tasks are not just done but done well. In the long run, quality builds trust. It creates reputations, secures loyalty, and sets a foundation that can withstand challenges. Speed fades quickly; excellence endures.

## The Habit of Mastery

Ultimately, execution excellence is not an occasional act but a habitual standard. It is the commitment to bring your best effort, whether the task is small or large, visible or unseen. The way you execute in the little things shapes how you perform in the big ones.

Over time, this consistency creates a reputation, one that says, *"This person delivers."* That reputation becomes one of your greatest assets, attracting opportunities, partnerships, and trust. Excellence is not about perfection; it is about dependability, integrity, and the relentless pursuit of better.

Execution, then, is not merely the final stage of the process; it is the stage that validates everything before it. Skills, tools, and strategies only matter if they are carried out with discipline, measured with intention, improved with curiosity, and performed with excellence.

# Section III. The Laws

As an owner of the state, you must be familiar with the strength of abiding by the law. And due to this, you live under the provisions of rules and regulations that control our society. Laws and regulations, therefore, serve as a barrier barring anarchy and the unifier of human relations. This is where we can agree on the issue, understanding and obeying the laws of the society, as making everything better. The third section of this potent productivity plan points out two laws in mathematics and one law in universality. These laws, along with the man-made laws, make you have the feeling that you belong to something bigger when you obey them. This sharing of these laws and gaining an understanding of their application will go a long way in helping the growth of organizations or individuals, and in many ways, this will increase the productivity of such people. I am aware of the existence of other laws that exist in our universe; however, these three laws are the ones that have the most bearing on the intention of being more productive.

# Chapter Seven: Law of Averages

I said to you earlier, I like numbers. I like to see them in statistical analysis, in analyses such as key performance indicators, in my balance sheets and in the case of this legislation, in averages.

When you do something equally on a repeated basis, you will get a figure or a ratio and end up having an average. The largest aspect of this average is that when it begins, it more or less continues. Example; when you engage in sales and you address ten clients during which one of them purchases your product, this means that your average = 0.1 or 10:1. This average will lead you to various good ways, as it was always asserted by Jim Rohn, when a person realizes how this law works he/she can score with numbers in areas where he/she lags in skills. In a short time, you will find that as you keep trying this law in your operations, your skills will improve upon and now your ratio or average may be 10:2.

In case you are a sports personality, you probably like averages, as they report to you on the quality of the performance of your favorite sportsmen. You should be able to interpret the law of averages through the eye of the sport industry, since you will find that you need not average

100 in order to be great. Grab a legendary three-point shooter like

Larry Bird, the greatest ever to shoot the ball and the best he has ever recorded, averagely just a bit higher than 45 percent.

## The Math of Success

The Law of Averages is one of the guiding philosophies of every individual who will need to realize a massive target. It takes the emotional aspect out of the equation and puts logic and a common reality that, as long as you do something enough times, you will eventually be a success. On this, the key to disappointment turns. Most human beings make one or two attempts at something new, fail and quit. They are yet unaware that they are just beginning to set their average.

Suppose you want to get the job of your dreams. You send five resumes and do not receive any reply. It might get discouraging. The Law of Averages will assuredly tell you that you simply have not yet made your figures. Your average could be 1, 50, i.e., 50 resumes sent, everyone calls back. When you understand this, then the rejection of the first 5 resumes should not be seen as a failure but a data point. It is just one of the procedures.

This legislation is an efficient anti-motivating weapon. When you are feeling discouraged and may want to quit, you can say to yourself, I have only called five people. In order to have one sale, I have to make fifty. I am not failing, I am still working on my GPA towards the middle.

**Increasing Your Average**

Here is the beautiful thing about such a law: Your average is not fixed. It is a dynamic, living figure and it can be affected by ability and effort. You may originally compensate for the absence of skill by mass. You may have to speak to ten people in order to close one sale. However, through an entire activity, you improve. You are taught how to be more effective when communicating, how to know your audience better and how to seal the deal. Your 10:1 gradually turns into 9:1, then 8:1, etc.

All the other ideas in this book--defined goals, checklists, and an SOP--also focus on enabling you to raise your average. Those are the instruments to take you out of a 10:1 ratio to a 2:1 ratio. As the Law of Average acts as the blank paper, your firm resolution and patience are the colours. Your success rate is under your control.

It is a business idea that goes beyond increasing business figures. This is applicable to all walks of life. Looking to better your health? Your mean may be the number of days you exercise in a week. Wish to learn a new language? Your average is the number of new words each day. The greater effort you expend, the more your average rises. The trick is to be steady and to monitor your success. Just keep in mind, what is measured is what will get managed.

# Chapter Eight: Law of Diminishing Intent

Although procrastination may be ascribed to many factors such as laziness, the loss of focus, or lack of awareness, this is the case. We may all agree that procrastination may harm your personal and/or professional growth.

The law of diminishing intent can inform us that the longer you keep doing something the more it is likely there is a likelihood that you will never do it. The delays may not be intentional, even though they impact your productivity. John Maxwell, my mentor, adds that when you have an idea but do not take any action within 48hours, chances are that you will never do it.

We know of the person who cannot find time to start taking action until Monday, which is the first of the month, and the least favorite of the New Year's resolutions.

**How to Fight the Diminishment**

The confusing clock of the Law of Diminishing Intent suggests that the momentum is your most important asset. A thought in your mind is nothing. It is not a fact until you do something about it. The more time you leave, the more the initial passion and motivation that inspired the idea run out of juice. The enthusiasm you had on Monday morning, trying to get into your new fitness routine, will not seem very strong by Wednesday evening. The secret is to do it when the fire is burning.

- **Remain motivated:** let someone say that motivation is like a shower, you need one each day. It is important to periodically check your progress. Motivation does not happen to someone; rather, it happens because of action.

- **Be purposeful in your WHY:** Self-awareness is the same as knowing why. Your WHY is simply your desire to do something and to tell you there is nothing more powerful than a clean WHY. As a U.S Army leader, it is a norm that I ask every new soldier joining my team the reason he or she joined the U.S Army because through this, the soldier will give me a better understanding of his or her purpose and assist me as a leader to lead accordingly.

About five years ago, I read a brilliant concept known as the seven levels of WHY. I included this section, as I think it not only helps one to find the actual cause of my first intention but also keeps one on a track of what he/she has to do. The seven levels of why is simple when one asks oneself a question why he or she wants to accomplish a given goal and each time one gives the answer why to the same question, one has to repeat it seven times.

## The 48-Hour Rule

John Maxwell proposes the 48-hour rule, which is the first-hand practice of this law. It is a light yet life-altering exercise: whenever you get an idea or thought that you find really good, do something about it within 48 hours. The act need not be very big. This may be as easy as putting it in writing in detail, doing five minutes of research, or sharing it with a friend. This minor, preliminary step gets the ball rolling and counters the tendency to forget about a good idea and to allow it to die of inactivity. The initial spark is what prevents the fire from going away.

The Law of Diminishing Intent is what makes people who claim to want to become writers never open a book, and why would-be entrepreneurs never start up their enterprises, and why so many New Year's resolutions go unfulfilled in the first month. Failure does not kill your dream; the dream kills itself by not being acted on.

## The "Do It Now" Principle

This law is an imperative. It is a timely reminder not to wait any longer to do something because there will never be a perfect time, or perfect resources, or perfect plan. The best moment to act is when there is a chance of doing it now. Consider the last excellent idea you came up with.

What has happened to clue? Or you might have it on a notepad, or it might be lingering in the back of your mind, or it might be on some to-do list that just keeps getting pushed back to tomorrow. Your fantastic ideas cannot be left as victims of your procrastination.

One way to make it is to introduce the Two-Minute Rule. When you have something to do that will take less than two minutes, do it immediately. Never include it in your to-do list; never contemplate it, never even think about it, simply do it. This basic guideline develops the habit of taking action and develops a sense of power in its momentum. It aids in probing your mind to have better clarity and concentrate your energy on doing the greater things that take time and effort. The sooner you do it now, the less you will have to do it later.

# Chapter Nine: Law, Cause, and Effect

This is one of the twelve universal laws and it is based on science as well as philosophy. In this case, we know that nothing occurs by chance. There is a cause to every effect and an effect to every cause. The law of cause and effect states that there exists a law that the effects of an action will be an equal and opposite reaction.

It is noteworthy to mention that this law is applicable in both the material world and the interaction of human behavior. We should also stress the meaning of intention. Apply the measures that are subject to the objectives that you desire. The Reaper shall gather.

## The Foundation of Intentionality

This law is the proverbial law of productivity. It also informs you that all the consequences you are experiencing in life, whether positive or negative, are one way or another, a direct product of a cause you initiated. What happens to your level of health can be traced to how you eat and exercise. Your economic status is a consequence of your financial behavior of either spending or saving. Your earning power is the by- product of the hours and efforts that you spend on learning and development. There is no luck in the long run. What you get is directly and inseparably connected to what you do.

This law makes it squarely your responsibility. It clears the excuses, and gives power to the truth that you are doing control. Provided you do not like the effects that you are getting, you must alter the causes. When you are not achieving the results you desire, the Law of Cause and Effect tells you to analyze your behaviors. Do your day-to-day activities agree with your long-term expectations? Are you working on what your dream demands?

**The Principle of the Sower**

Transplanting will reap the sower." These few words are among the richest in this law. It is an indication that what you did not sow will not be harvested by you. When you plant fruit flowers, you get fruit flowers. You cannot plant thistles and sow roses. Similarly, you cannot put in laziness and procrastination and expect to harvest success.

What you do every day is actually what you are planting seeds in life.

- Those seeds of involved work, discipline, and constant learning will bear the fruit of success.

- Indecisiveness, distraction, and non-consideration will plant the roots of mediocrity and entail wasted growth.

The garden is your life, and you are the Sower. This legislation reminds us at all times that what you hope to have in the future is being created, or not being created, by what you do now.

Impact is the final measure of all growth. Skills provide the foundation, tools bring efficiency, laws offer guidance, and actions generate momentum. Growth stretches these elements into maturity, and legacy preserves them across time. But impact transcends even legacy, it is where all of these converge into something greater than the self. It is the stage where your journey ceases to be only about you and begins to alter the course of others, communities, and even generations.

Impact is not defined by visibility. It is not the trophies on the shelf, the applause of the crowd, or the wealth accumulated along the way. True impact is quieter, deeper, and more enduring. It is measured by transformation: how a person's life shifts because of your influence, how a family is strengthened by your example, how an environment is improved because of your contributions, how the future bends in a new direction because of the structures you set in motion.

Without impact, success risks becoming shallow, a victory contained within the walls of the self. It is achievement without extension, progress without purpose. But with impact, success evolves into significance. It stretches beyond individual goals and accomplishments to create change that others can inherit, build upon, and expand. Impact answers the question: *What did my growth make possible for someone else?*

Impact is rarely instant. It often begins invisibly, in the unseen spaces where influence is first planted. A single conversation may alter the way someone sees themselves. A single system may raise standards for an entire organization. A single principle lived consistently can inspire generations. Like ripples in water, the smallest action, when rooted in values, expands outward far beyond what you may ever witness.

This stage represents a profound transformation of perspective. No longer is the focus on climbing your own mountain. Instead, the climb becomes a platform to help others ascend. Victory shifts from being personal to being shared. What once was about proving yourself now becomes about improving others. The questions deepen:

*How can what I've built serve beyond me?*
*What do others gain from my journey?*

*What would not exist if I had not acted?*

Impact, then, is not an event but an orientation. It is a way of living where growth naturally turns outward, where strength becomes service, and where achievement multiplies into abundance for others.

At its highest form, impact becomes generational. What you set in place today may shape decisions and possibilities for people you will never meet, in times you will never see. A principle you uphold could guide an industry. A value you defend could redefine a culture. A system you design could protect people long after your name is forgotten. In this way, impact is larger than recognition it is contribution made permanent.

Ultimately, impact is what gives life its deepest meaning. Achievements may fade. Possessions may pass. But the lives you've touched, the culture you've influenced, the standards you've raised, and the future you've helped construct endure. Impact is the proof that your existence mattered, not only to you but to the world.

## Service Beyond Self

Impact begins with service. Growth becomes meaningful only when it overflows into others. Service beyond self is the practice of turning personal gain into collective benefit, of using your resources, knowledge, and strength to lift others higher. It is the shift from accumulation to contribution, from "What can I get?" to "What can I give?"

True service is not charity that comes from abundance alone; it is responsibility. It is recognizing that the measure of your success is not just what you achieved but how many you helped achieve. It is giving not only from what you have, but also from who you are.

Service creates ripple effects. A single act of generosity inspires others to give. A single mentor shapes generations through the lives of their students. Service multiplies because it plants seeds in people who then carry them forward.

For service to become transformative, however, it must move beyond moments of kindness and become a philosophy of life.

## The Shift from Self to Others

At the beginning of any journey, survival and personal growth are the natural focus. You work to establish stability, build competence, and secure opportunities. But when growth matures, it asks a bigger question: *What now?*

The answer is service.

Shifting from self to others requires a conscious reframing:

**From scarcity to abundance.** Instead of clinging to what you have, you believe there is enough to share and that sharing creates more.

**From competition to contribution.** Instead of measuring your value against others, you measure your worth by what you bring to them.

**From achievement to alignment.** Instead of stopping at "I won," you ask, "Who else did my win benefit?"

This shift does not subtract from your success. It multiplies it. You gain by giving, not because of material returns, but because your growth now carries meaning beyond yourself.

**Forms of Service: Beyond the Obvious**

Service takes many shapes, not all of them financial. Some of the most enduring forms of service are often invisible:

**Time:** Sitting with someone in their struggle, teaching patiently, mentoring steadily, and being present when presence matters most.

**Knowledge:** Passing on lessons learned, helping others avoid mistakes you've made, equipping them with wisdom that accelerates their journey.

**Resources:** Sharing opportunities, tools, or connections that open doors others could not access on their own.

**Character**: Modeling integrity, resilience, and kindness. Sometimes, what you embody inspires more than anything you say or give.

**Encouragement**: Believing in someone when they cannot yet believe in themselves.

Often, what seems small to you an encouraging word, a simple piece of advice, a bit of your time can become life-changing to someone else.

## Service as Responsibility, Not Luxury

Many delay service, believing it should come "later" after success, after wealth, after recognition. But this perspective mistakes service for luxury. In reality, service is responsibility.

Your skills, resources, and opportunities are not yours alone. They are entrusted to you, and with that trust comes the duty to use them for others. To grow without giving is to hoard; to grow and give is to honor the purpose of growth.

Service becomes the validation of your journey. It proves your growth has value, not only for you but for the world around you.

## The Ripple Effect of Service

The beauty of service lies in its multiplication. Unlike achievements, which often remain personal, acts of service reverberate outward.

A teacher shapes not only students but also the countless lives those students will later touch.

A business leader who values fairness may raise the ethical standards of an entire industry.

A single act of compassion in a community may inspire movements that transform society.

The ripple often outlives the original act. You may never see the full circle of your service, but its effects continue long after you are gone.

## The Paradox of Service: The Giver is Enriched

One of life's paradoxes is that in giving, we are not diminished but enriched. Service does not weaken you; it strengthens you. It enlarges your capacity for empathy, sharpens your sense of purpose, and deepens your fulfillment.

**Giving time** clarifies what really matters.

**Sharing knowledge** cements your own understanding.

**Offering resources** strengthens your stewardship and gratitude.

**Living with integrity** enhances your own sense of meaning.

In serving others, you stretch yourself. You discover capacities you did not know you had, and you find joy in contributions that no personal achievement could match.

**Sustainable Service: Building it into Life**

For service to be effective, it must be sustainable. Burning yourself out benefits no one. Building a life of service requires balance:

**Intentionality**: Look for ways to serve daily, not just when it's convenient.

**Consistency**: Make service habitual, not seasonal.

**Balance:** Serve from your strengths, but also protect your well-being. Giving is sustainable only when rooted in health.

**Alignment:** Serve in ways consistent with your values and skills, so service feels natural, not forced.

When service is woven into your way of life, it becomes effortless. It shifts from being something you "do" to something you "are."

**From Acts to Atmosphere**

The highest form of service is not an occasional act but an atmosphere. It is creating environments where others naturally feel valued, supported, and uplifted.

In leadership, this means cultivating cultures where people grow.

In family, it means building homes where love and encouragement are normal.

In community, it means fostering spaces where collective strength thrives.

An atmosphere of service magnifies impact because it moves beyond moments into culture. It sets a tone that continues even in your absence.

**The Enduring Power of Service**

Service ensures that what you have built does not end with you. It is the bridge between your growth and the world's progress. Without service, even great achievements risk fading quickly. With service, even the smallest act can echo for generations.

When you serve, you plant seeds that grow into trees you may never sit under. You water futures you may never see. And yet, those unseen results become your truest impact.

Service beyond self is not just an act of kindness. It is the highest expression of maturity, the deepest form of strength, and the clearest path to significance.

## Cultural Contribution The Imprint of Every Life

Every life leaves an imprint on culture, whether intentionally or unconsciously. Culture is not only the domain of nations or corporations, it exists in every family, team, organization, and community. Wherever people gather, culture forms. It is the shared way of thinking, speaking, and acting that silently guides behavior, the unspoken atmosphere that either lifts people higher or pulls them down. Cultural contribution, therefore, is not optional. Each person plays a role, whether by shaping the culture intentionally or by allowing it to drift into patterns of mediocrity and neglect. The real question is not whether you will contribute to culture, but what kind of culture you will leave behind.

## The Invisible Force of Culture

Culture is often unseen, yet it is always present. It acts like the air in a room, unnoticed until it grows stale or toxic, but essential for life. It is the invisible architect behind visible outcomes, the quiet force that makes excellence possible or that permits decay. Culture is expressed in the unspoken rules people live by, in the atmosphere you feel when you walk into a workplace, a classroom, or a household, and in the collective habits that determine what gets done, how it gets done, and why it gets done. Unlike commands or regulations, which require enforcement, culture is self-reinforcing. People adapt to culture more quickly than they obey rules, which is why culture holds such power over behavior and outcomes.

## The Role of the Individual

The influence of the individual on culture is often underestimated. Many assume that only leaders or institutions shape culture, but the truth is that every single person contributes to it every day. The tone of a single conversation, the way criticism is delivered, the decision to encourage rather than dismiss, all of these actions are cultural contributions. In a family, if parents consistently choose patience over anger, they build a culture of safety and trust that their children carry into adulthood. In a workplace, if one employee models excellence, it raises expectations for everyone else, proving that the standard is possible. In a community, if neighbors choose connection instead of isolation, they set a tone of belonging that makes others feel valued. Every action, repeated over time, becomes part of the DNA of the environment we inhabit.

## Unintentional vs. Intentional Contribution

The danger, however, is that most culture is shaped by accident. Left unchecked, environments often slip into negativity, mediocrity, and cynicism. When cultural contribution is unintentional, gossip spreads, dishonesty grows, and apathy becomes the norm. Intentional cultural contribution requires awareness and commitment. It is the choice to counter these destructive forces with encouragement, integrity, and accountability, even when doing so costs something. The question is never whether you are influencing culture; the question is always whether you are shaping it by design or permitting it by neglect.

## The Building Blocks of Culture

Culture is not built in a day; it is built in patterns. Certain mechanisms make culture tangible and enduring. Values must be lived, not simply stated, because people trust what they see more than what they hear. Stories told and retold also shape culture families, organizations, and nations are defined by the narratives they celebrate, whether of sacrifice, triumph, or resilience. Rituals and traditions further cement identity, as shared practices reinforce belonging and continuity. And above all, culture is revealed not by lofty mission statements but by what is rewarded and what is tolerated. Excellence grows when it is recognized, while mediocrity thrives when it is allowed to pass unchallenged. These mechanisms values, stories, rituals, rewards form the building blocks of any culture.

## The Ripple Effect of Culture

The ripple of culture is powerful and far-reaching. A single person's consistent contribution can echo through time. A teacher who sets high expectations may influence not only her students but the countless lives those students later touch. A business founder who insists on fairness may create a culture that employees feel proud of decades later. A parent who models resilience and kindness can set a tone for generations of children who inherit that mindset. Cultural contribution, once established, is one of the rare investments that compounds across people, places, and time.

## The Cost of Neglect

But just as positive contribution multiplies, so too does neglect. Cultures do not drift upward by chance; they degrade unless they are actively cultivated. In families, neglect breeds resentment, distance, and silence. In organizations, neglect produces politics, dishonesty, and disengagement. In societies, neglect allows corruption, injustice, and division to flourish. What is tolerated today becomes tomorrow's norm, and once a toxic pattern takes root, it is difficult to reverse. This is why cultural contribution is not a luxury but a necessity without it, decline is inevitable.

## Culture as Legacy

Cultural contribution is also one of the most enduring forms of legacy. Material possessions eventually fade, structures crumble, and names are forgotten, but culture outlasts them all. Nations carry the spirit of their founders, whether good or bad. Companies maintain the vision of their earliest builders long after leadership changes. Families hold on to traditions, values, and practices passed down by ancestors who may no longer be remembered by name but who still live through the atmosphere they created. In this way, cultural contribution is not only about immediate influence but about shaping a future you may never see.

## Practical Pathways to Contribution

To contribute positively to culture requires intention. It means modeling daily values with consistency, knowing that others are watching even when you think they are not. It means telling meaningful stories that remind people of victories, resilience, and shared purpose, keeping hope alive. It means establishing rituals and standards, understanding that repeated practices anchor culture more effectively than speeches. It means correcting drift when it appears, refusing to allow toxic behaviors to define the environment. And it means thinking generationally, asking: *If this culture lasts beyond me, would I be proud of it?*

## The Lasting Question

Cultural contribution is one of the most powerful and enduring forms of impact. It outlasts wealth, possessions, and personal achievements. It exists in the atmosphere people breathe long after you are gone. Your contribution may seem small today, a word of encouragement, a standard upheld,, a tradition continued, but collectively, these actions shape the environments where people live, work, and grow. The culture you contribute to today will shape lives tomorrow. The truth is, every life leaves a cultural imprint. The only question is: *What kind of culture will you leave behind?*

## The Future You Create Shaping Tomorrow Through Today

The future is not something that simply arrives on its own, it is something we actively construct through our actions, decisions, and values. Every word spoken, every choice made, every priority embraced is a brick in the foundation of tomorrow. Some of these bricks will be visible in our own lifetime, producing outcomes we can enjoy and measure, while others will remain hidden, forming structures that only future generations will stand upon. When we think of the future, it is easy to imagine it as something distant and abstract, but in truth, it is being created moment by moment in the present. Each step you take today either strengthens or weakens the foundation of tomorrow. This means that the future is not a matter of chance but of responsibility, it belongs to those who recognize the weight of their influence and act accordingly.

## The Power of Small Choices

It is tempting to believe that the future is determined by dramatic moments, world-changing inventions, major political shifts, or bold public acts of leadership. But in reality, the shape of the future is carved mostly by smaller, quieter decisions that accumulate over time. Choosing honesty when dishonesty seems easier, extending kindness when indifference is more convenient, or committing to discipline when distraction tempts you may feel insignificant in the moment. Yet repeated consistently, these small decisions form habits, and habits shape character. Character, in turn, defines destiny. Just as the steady dripping of water can hollow out stone or the daily rise of the sun reshapes the growth of a tree, it is the small, consistent actions that define the contours of the future. One healthy habit can rewrite the trajectory of your life; one courageous stand can redirect the course of an entire community. The truth is, the future is never built in leaps but in steady steps, and what you choose to do repeatedly carries far more weight than what you do occasionally.

## The Long Shadow of Influence

The future you create extends far beyond yourself. Every human life casts a shadow that stretches into the lives of others, sometimes in ways you may never see or fully understand. A parent, for example, shapes the future of their children not merely through advice but through the environment they cultivate, the security, encouragement, or pressure they provide becomes the soil in which those children grow. A leader in an organization may retire or move on, but the systems, standards, and values they leave behind continue to influence the culture for decades. An innovator's breakthrough can redefine industries, altering how millions of people work, live, and interact with the world. This ripple effect means your actions are never isolated, they are threads woven into a much larger fabric of influence. The danger of forgetting this truth is that we may underestimate our responsibility, dismissing our role as small or irrelevant. But in reality, the smallest acts of courage, integrity, or neglect often produce consequences far beyond what we can measure in the present. You are never creating your future alone, you are always shaping the collective future with every decision you make.

## Vision and Responsibility

No one stumbles into a meaningful future by accident. Futures that endure and inspire are always crafted with vision and responsibility. Vision is the ability to see beyond the immediate, to imagine realities not yet visible, and to hold in your heart a picture of what could be. It is the compass that keeps you from drifting aimlessly, the light that guides you through seasons of uncertainty. Responsibility is the discipline of aligning your actions with that vision, of doing the work even when recognition is absent and the results are slow. Without vision, the future collapses into a cycle of reacting to circumstances rather than creating them. Without responsibility, vision dissolves into empty daydreams. When the two come together, however, the effect is powerful, vision directs your aim, while responsibility builds the road that gets you there. The most transformative futures belong to those who are courageous enough to imagine boldly but humble enough to work diligently.

## Breaking Free from the Present

One of the greatest obstacles in creating the future is the magnetic pull of the present. The demands of today, immediate deadlines, daily routines, and personal comforts, often overshadow the importance of tomorrow. People cling to what is familiar, even if it is limiting, because the uncertainty of change feels uncomfortable. Comfort, fear, and habit act as invisible anchors, keeping individuals and societies tied to the present when the horizon beckons them forward. To build the future, one must develop the courage to step beyond what is known, to invest in actions that may not yield immediate results, and to trust in processes that require patience. It requires shifting your perspective from *"What do I gain right now?"* to *"What am I setting in motion that will matter long after this moment?"* Just as farmers sow seeds in one season and wait months or years for the harvest, builders of the future must be willing to act for outcomes they may not fully enjoy themselves. Those who overcome the gravity of the present are the ones who redefine what is possible for the generations that follow.

## The Generational Dimension

The future you create is rarely confined to your own lifetime. What you build, protect, or neglect becomes the starting point for others. Every generation inherits systems, traditions, and opportunities, some strong and empowering, others weak and broken. A teacher's influence may live on for decades through the lives of students who carry forward her lessons and pass them on to their children. A business founder may never meet the employees hired decades later, but their decision to prioritize fairness or innovation still shapes the environment those workers step into. A parent's choice to model resilience or kindness can echo across generations, producing a lineage defined by strength, compassion, or vision. Each generation is both a product of the past and a steward of the future, holding in its hands the responsibility to either repair what was broken or multiply what was good. When you act, you are not only living for yourself but shaping the inheritance of people you may never meet.

## The Weight of Inaction

Just as deliberate action creates the future, so too does inaction. Neglect is not neutral, it is destructive. Ignoring a problem does not make it disappear; it only allows it to grow more dangerous. Delaying a decision does not keep the future at bay; it merely surrenders control to chance. Refusing to grow does not preserve the present; it guarantees decline. The future punishes apathy as surely as it rewards intentionality. A garden left untended will fill with weeds, a structure left unrepaired will eventually collapse, and a society that refuses to confront its challenges will crumble under their weight. Inaction is not simply a pause in progress, it is a decision that transfers the cost to someone else, often to the next generation. This truth may feel heavy, but it is also liberating, because it means that every small step of intentional action matters. Every act of courage, however modest, is a way of reclaiming the future from the grip of neglect.

## A Future Worth Building

Ultimately, the future you create reflects the values you hold most deeply. If you value comfort above all, you may build a life of stability but little growth. If you value growth, you will create opportunity but must also embrace resilience, for growth always carries struggle. If you value contribution, you will build significance that outlives you, touching lives beyond your reach. The key is to ask yourself with honesty: *What future do I want to be responsible for?* Because whether you plan it or not, you are building a future every day. The question is not whether you will create one, but whether it will be one worth inheriting. Your future, and the future of others, is always in motion, always taking shape. The responsibility and privilege of life is to shape it intentionally, to leave behind not just traces of existence but pathways of possibility.

# Final Thoughts

And whether you craved to read this book to find out more on how to achieve more results, I hope I have covered enough and you are off to your journey of getting more results. I have personally tested the nine concepts discussed with you. My own life and career achievements are, in one way, directly attributable to the philosophy contained herein.

My greatest goal is that you have acquired the knowledge to be able to structure different types of strategies by combining these nine concepts. And neither would this be a magic book, as any other book containing information of value; there would be no effect as soon as one started reading it. You will have to take some tremendous action towards what you have just learnt and make sure that you adapt these skills, tools and laws so that they will work in your favor and your team.

**Develop Practical Tools Section**

It does not matter how much or how little you understand the concepts; what matters is how you apply the concepts in your everyday life. It is putting a system that works in balance. Pause to consider what you have learned and how you can use it in order to take effect now.

- **Law of Average:** What is your current average in one important aspect of your life, whether you make sales calls, job applications, or workout sessions? Write it out. But what is one small step you can take to bump up that average by half a percentage point at a time?

- **The Law of Diminishing Intent:** What is one great idea you have had in the past 48 hours that you have not done anything about? Write it down, do something small and incremental on it now. Waiting on motivation is a waste of time; instead, create it.

- **The Law of Cause and Effect:** How do you feel about one of the things that is the effect of your life? What cause has produced it? What can you do yourself about that beginning today?

Your call to action is these questions. They are the medium between the knowledge and application. Now that you have read the words, perhaps it is time to put them into action.

More output, more achievement, more fulfilled existence is a marathon rather than a sprint. It is something that requires discipline, requires commitment, and this is something that has to be constantly applied to these laws, skills and tools.

Your world is waiting for your work. Start now, and look not behind. The results are yours to take.

## The Power of Perpetual Learning

Finally, with this concluding journey, I want to leave you with one final concept that bridges together the 9 concepts that I have shared and this concept is perpetual learning. The world is in flux. Every day, new technologies, new markets, and new challenges are created. The skills, tools and laws you have learnt are eternal and their usage must change.

A proficient project manager does not live on the knowledge that he had yesterday. They read, are always studying and learning through their experiences. The disciplined person is not only oriented to the current task, but she or he is oriented towards the future prospects. The Law of Average, the Law of Diminishing Intent and the Law of Cause and Effect all operate to your advantage only as long as you are in a state of continuous improvement.

Your drive is to learn and develop and that is what powers your productive machine. This is the one habit of any kind that you need to cultivate most of all and as you go out there and you start to use these principles in the world, be sure to be curious, be sure to be humble, be sure to always learn something new. Your prospects are unlimited. It is just that you have to be willing to work towards it.

## The Ripple Effect of Action

The Law of Cause and Effect can also be used in indirect consequences. It also extends to the nuanced and long-reaching impact of what you do- the ripple effect. One small act of kindness has the power to make a person feel good about their day and this increases the chances of that person helping another person. In the same way, one mistake of carelessness can trigger a chain of adverse events. Intentionality plays this important role; therefore, any decision you make, any action you take, has a ripple effect in your life and the lives of other people. You are not only defining your own future; you are throwing some light into the world around you.

This requires one to be really thoughtful about what to do. You cannot merely do it as a habit or as an instinct. Take action. Ask yourself, what do I really want to have happen? What is the most important thing I can do right now to make this happen? Such a kind of thinking ties your every action to your final objectives and does not leave a chance to spend even the smallest moment.

# Conclusion: Living in Peak Mode

Every journey has a starting point, and yours began the moment you picked up this book. Perhaps you opened it because you felt overwhelmed by the pace of life. Perhaps you were tired of working hard but seeing little progress. Or maybe you wanted to sharpen your edge, to discover practical ways to multiply your results without multiplying your stress.

Now, after moving through these pages, you stand at a different point. You've been introduced to a framework that is not abstract theory, but a set of practical tools designed to transform the way you live and work. You now understand that productivity is not about being busy; it is about being effective. It is not about filling every hour; it is about filling the right hours with the right actions.

**Peak Mode is not a destination. It is a way of living. What You've Learned**

Over the course of this book, you've walked through **nine tactical concepts** that build on one another like steps in a ladder:

- **The Skills** (Goal Setting, Time Usage, and Project Management) gave you the foundation. They are the personal competencies that ensure your efforts are directed, disciplined, and sustainable.

- **The Tools** (Checklists, SOPs, KPIs) gave you the structure. They turn ideas into systems, reducing guesswork and replacing chaos with clarity.

- **The Laws** (Averages, Diminishing Intent, Cause and Effect) gave you the truth. They remind you that results don't come by accident, they are governed by principles that never change.

Each of these areas serves a unique purpose. Skills shape your behavior, tools shape your process, and laws shape your mindset. Together, they create alignment, an operating system for your personal and professional life.

Think of it this way: without skills, you lack direction. Without tools, you lack structure. Without laws, you lack perspective. But when all three are in harmony, you unlock the ability to consistently perform at your best.

That's **Peak Mode.**

## Beyond Productivity: The Bigger Picture

At first glance, this book may have seemed like it was only about getting more done. But look closer, and you'll see it is about much more. It is about freedom, the freedom to take control of your days instead of being controlled by them. It is about clarity, the ability to separate what truly matters from what only seems urgent. And it is about growth, the kind of growth that doesn't just improve your results, but improves your life.

Productivity is not just about money, output, or efficiency. It is about designing a life that reflects your values. It is about creating the capacity to spend time with your loved ones, to serve your community, to pursue your passions, and to leave a legacy that matters.

When you live in **Peak Mode**, you don't just achieve more, you become more.

## The Cost of Inaction

Before you close this book and move on, I need to be clear about something. Knowledge alone will not change your life. Understanding these concepts is only the first step. If you do not act, nothing will change.

Every day you delay is a day of lost potential. Every hour wasted on distractions is an hour you could have invested in building your future. Every opportunity missed because of procrastination is a seed of regret planted in tomorrow.

Imagine yourself five years from now. If you ignore what you've learned, you'll likely find yourself in the same place, or worse, further behind. But if you apply even a fraction of these principles, you could be living in a completely different reality: financially stronger, emotionally freer, more focused, and more fulfilled.

The cost of inaction is always higher than the cost of discipline.

**Moving Forward: Your Next Steps**

So what comes next? The answer is simple: *start small, but start now.*

1. **Choose one concept.** Don't try to implement all nine at once. Pick one, maybe SMART goals, or time blocking, or micro-goals, and make it a habit.

2. **Track your progress.** Productivity compounds. The small wins you celebrate today will turn into breakthroughs tomorrow.

3. **Stay accountable.** Find a mentor, coach, or accountability partner who won't let you drift.

4. **Revisit this book often.** Think of it as a manual. When you feel stuck, return to the chapter that matches your challenge.

5. **Build your 90-day plan.** Commit to applying these principles for the next three months. By day 90, you will notice a measurable difference in your results.

Remember: success doesn't happen in one leap, it happens in consistent steps.

## Legacy and Impact

One of the most powerful truths about productivity is this: it is contagious. When you operate in Peak Mode, you inspire others to do the same. Your team begins to model your clarity. Your family benefits from your presence. Your community is strengthened by your contributions.

Productivity is not just about what you achieve, it is about what you enable others to achieve. The systems you build, the values you uphold, and the example you set will outlive you. That is how you leave a legacy.

And ultimately, legacy is the greatest productivity of all, multiplying your impact far beyond your own lifetime.

## One Final Reminder

This book may be ending, but your journey is just beginning. The path to Peak Mode is lifelong. There will be days when you stumble, when distractions win, or when you feel like you're slipping back into old habits. That's normal. The key is not perfection, its persistence.

Each time you refocus, each time you recommit, you are proving to yourself that you are capable of living at your best. And each day you choose Peak Mode, you are one step closer to becoming the person you were meant to be.

So ask yourself:

- Will I drift into the future, or will I design it?

- Will I let time control me, or will I control my time?

- Will I settle for average mode, or will I rise into **Peak Mode**?

The choice is yours.

Now go, take what you've learned, apply it with courage, and live in Peak Mode. The world is waiting for the results only you can create.

# THE END